WINNING
YOUR
AUDIENCE

WINNING
YOUR
AUDIENCE

Deliver a Message
with the Confidence of
a President

JAMES ROSEBUSH

**CENTER
STREET**

NASHVILLE NEW YORK

Center Street
Hachette Book Group
1290 Avenue of the Americas, New York, NY 10104
centerstreet.com
twitter.com/centerstreet

First Edition: April 2020

Center Street is a division of Hachette Book Group, Inc. The Center Street name and logo are trademarks of Hachette Book Group, Inc.

The publisher is not responsible for websites (or their content) that are not owned by the publisher.

Library of Congress Control Number: 2020930112

ISBNs: 978-1-5460-8596-6 (hardcover), 978-1-5460-8595-9 (ebook)

Printed in the United States of America

LSC-H

10 9 8 7 6 5 4 3 2 1

Of all the talents bestowed upon men, none is so precious as the gift of oratory. He who enjoys it wields a power more durable than that of a great king. He is an independent force in the world.

From *The Scaffolding of Rhetoric*

by Winston Churchill

Contents

CONTENTS

CHAPTER FOUR
Defeating Fear

CHAPTER FIVE
Building a Bridge to Your Audience

CHAPTER SIX
Crossing the Bridge to Your Audience

CONTENTS

CHAPTER SEVEN
Own the Room with Storytelling

CHAPTER EIGHT
The Perfect Trifecta: Audience, Content, Delivery

CHAPTER NINE
The Architecture of a Great Speech

CHAPTER TEN
The Physical Delivery of Your Message

CONTENTS

CHAPTER ELEVEN
The Winning Send-Off

Introduction

Public speaking is the most common and requisite skill for which we receive the least amount of training.

I wrote this book for you. As you read and study this book and practice its principles, you will become an accomplished speaker and win your audience. It is likely that you are a part of the 75 percent of the global population who are afraid of speaking in public. This includes princes and prime ministers, presidents and preachers. It also includes students, salespeople, parents, managers, philanthropists, factory workers, and just about anyone who is required or chooses to communicate with other people. Prime Minister Margaret Thatcher, one of the most composed, powerful, and self-assured world leaders of all time, told me once that at times even she was afraid on the podium. To imagine that a woman with all that worldly experience could be fearful of speaking in public explains why the humblest among us also grows nervous at the prospect of being called upon to stand and deliver in front of an audience.

For many of us this means that deploying even the most basic communication skills, like making a phone call, can be challenging. Not surprisingly, there is a name for this fear and affliction: glossophobia. This book is designed to help you conquer fear and free your ego of the constraints that may keep you on the sidelines and from having success speaking in public. As you read this book, learn from its examples, and adopt and practice the critical skills you learn, you will find yourself growing in self-confidence and success. There is nothing more personally affirming than gaining dominion in public speaking. It will affect all aspects of your life, because learning to speak effectively rests on gaining new levels of self-knowledge and personal confidence. It's a game changer. I know this is true because it is how I started to unleash my own abilities. Let me tell you the story.

A few decades ago, as I walked the streets of Moscow in frigid midwinter, a perma-haze of low gray clouds dimming the atmosphere, I was aware that I was neither alone nor invisible. The intelligence agents assigned to trail me, admittedly a very low-value target, were not the elegant and shadowy figures I had seen in spy movies any more than the fat old women posted inside the hotels, "Babas" as they were called, were grandmotherly. These worn-out elderly "hosts" always collected my room key when I went out and held it until I returned for a night's sleep at the formerly grand, and by then faded, National Hotel—a five-minute walk from Red Square and Lenin's tomb. They said that they pocketed my keys so they could "clean" the room while I was out.

As I walked the streets, in between meetings with government officials, it was damp and freezing cold and yet it was hard to stop watching the mesmerizingly efficient mechanized removal of ever-present snow being cleared from the broad boulevards and then dumped into the Moscow River.

I imagined this to be a massive socialist snow-removing operation far different than the haphazard snow shoveling near the Flint River, in the industrial Midwestern town where I was raised, which is now known more for its contaminated public water supply than its storied past as a major automotive manufacturing hub.

As a Rotary International Scholar, I had been invited to the Soviet Union at age twenty-one to conduct face-to-face meetings with ranking government officials who were three times my age and four times my girth. In America, I was just a budding philanthropic executive, and it took all my self-confidence to pretend I was talking to my equals and to hold conversations of substance through ever-present interpreters. The images of numerous Moscow meetings in massive communist office blocks, and in Leningrad's more traditional historic buildings where our meetings were held, have never left me. While the meetings were all planned and orchestrated for me, I was left on my own to conduct them. Communication was challenging but ultimately informative and rewarding.

In the evenings I found cultural events and museums to visit. More than once I risked being noticed by the police when I agreed to tutor strangers who begged me to teach them English. I used a few books I had stowed away in my suitcase to train them, which was a violation of my visa conditions. I am not sure I understood the potential cost of my youthful indiscretions, and I was certain to have warranted the creation of a thin surveillance dossier of some kind. The next time I would negotiate with Soviet officials came a decade later when I was working for President Ronald Reagan. These meetings included their own measure of intrigue.

After three weeks of meetings in Moscow and Leningrad on this first trip, I boarded a Russian Aeroflot 747 jet bound for New York, complete with farmers holding their highly excited caged chickens as well as cold cuts and vodka—which they shared liberally with their fellow travelers. Now I faced something more frightening than my meetings with the portly communists I had become acquainted with on my trip, or the tinge of terror I felt flying across the Atlantic on a rickety plane with boisterous Russians.

Once I arrived back in the US from the Soviet Union, it was my responsibility to give a speech to the Rotary Club about my experience. The good news was that my dad was a Dale Carnegie speech instructor, and I had been his student. The bad news was that he would be in the audience to judge, and possibly inhibit, my performance. This would not be the first time I would suffer from his severe critique of my speaking skills. He was the master teacher, and I was less than a master student. I had learned and practiced the basic principles of the then-famous Dale Carnegie training—thinking and imagining key points, tricks of memorization, dramatic storytelling, and more. Contemplating the task ahead, I thought about the perils of not presenting well.

Making every effort to turn fear into positive energy, I began to realize just how important storytelling and communicating are to history, scientific discoveries, and human progress. I also began to imagine, for the first time, the power of my own voice and its potential to educate and enlighten the audience about conditions in Soviet Russia. After all, this was no ordinary tourist trip. For once I knew I had stories to tell, and they were plentiful, colorful, and controversial. This gave me the courage to surmount my insecurities and to relate compelling and picturesque tales in a speech that received an enthusiastic response from the audience—including from my dad.

Years later, I found myself on an auditorium stage where Ronald Reagan had had a similar experience when he was near the same age I had been on my trip to Moscow. For Reagan this was the place where he first discovered the power of his voice to win his audience—even though it was decades later before he officially entered politics. As a freshman at Eureka College, in rural Illinois, where Abraham Lincoln, our sixteenth president, had spoken during his first presidential campaign, Reagan, later to be our fortieth president, was an unlikely organizer of a student strike. It was the students' goal to oust the president of the college, Bert Wilson, for his role in cutting the school budget at the onset of the Great Depression, thus eliminating popular courses at the college. In the vast, wood-floored, undistinguished gathering place for the school, then called the chapel, though not resembling one, Reagan launched his very first "political" campaign.

As he rose to speak, he had a full indictment of the school's president in hand and he recited the man's long list of failures as a leader. He was startled when his speech was interrupted with applause from his classmates. He later wrote of this occasion:

Giving that speech—my first—was as exciting as any I ever gave. For the first time in my life, I felt my words reach out and grab an audience, and it was exhilarating. When I'd say something, they'd roar after every

sentence, sometimes every word, and after a while, it
was as if the audience and I were one. When I called
for a vote on the strike, everybody rose to their feet
with a thunderous clapping of hands and approved
the proposal for a strike, by acclamation.

In fact, Reagan's description of his very first speech and
the audience reaction sounds more like what happens at a
Donald Trump rally than the way we remember Reagan's distinguished and relatively calm and grandfatherly perorations
as an American president. Both Trump and Reagan, in their
speeches, grasp the importance and value of being in a syn-
chronous cadence with their audience, feeding them what they
want to hear, and driving to an outcome or an important takeaway. Every speech for both leaders has been a value play—
Reagan's designed to achieve policy gains, and Trump's more
political.

Trump is a master at knowing his audience, having absolute confidence in his beliefs, defining good and evil, using
repetition, and being consistent, loud, and simple in his use of
words. These tactics have won him loyalty and large, boisterous crowds that show excitement about his points of view and
appreciation for his sticking with them. A friend of mine who
has been in Trump's audiences told me that she likes his bold
and direct word choices because "he is verbalizing what I am
thinking and yet reticent to say myself. President Trump does
it for me." The impact of those plain-speaking words of Trump
is intentional and is not lost on the media and the broader
audience in general.

This book focuses on the spoken word and its effective

delivery in any format—webinar and podcast presenter, *Shark Tank* competitor, political candidate, introducer, Toastmaster, preacher, professor, YouTube or TikTok videographer, TEDx inspirer, and professional lecturer. It is designed for every person who needs or desires to become an inspiring, impactful, and productive speaker, whether a salesperson, student in a classroom discussion or defending a dissertation, or a corporate leader who is participating in a stressful media interview following an oil spill, an airline crash, or failing corporate earnings.

My goal is to help every speaker win their audience and to achieve a desirable outcome, leaving the audience better educated, informed, or more inspired for having made the effort. This book includes a detailed guide to every conceivable element critical to effective public speaking; an assessment of the dynamic and highly competitive marketplace for presenters and speakers today; the historic and fundamental rules of rhetoric and examples of how these can be learned and applied; practical tools for performance; and stories about and examples of memorable presentations.

The original art of public speaking, called rhetoric, was introduced in ancient Greece largely for political purposes and to support embryonic steps to establish a democratic government. Down through the centuries oratory has been expressed and employed most in fields of education, law, religion, business, and politics. Because of the interrelationship of oratory, politics, and democracy, I have interwoven into my instruction and coaching in this book examples and stories about the crucial things I learned from my boss Ronald Reagan during my years at the White House. I have also included my analysis of President Trump's style and practice of communicating—a style that reflects the disruptive patterns and practices introduced by social media platforms and their effect on public speaking. Other noted leaders, some of whom I have met, and their own stories make appearances throughout this book to help us achieve our goals based on their examples.

My hope is that you will use this book like a handbook or field guide. Write in its margins. Highlight passages to return to. Tear out or copy pages. Make it a workhorse for you. Its design is to show you how to bring you, the speaker, and your audience together for a specific purpose or desired outcome. After you master these precepts, you should leave your audience wanting to hear more from you and appreciative that you made the effort.

If I have failed to answer any question you might have about presenting or speaking, please email me at jsrosebush @impactspeakercoach.com and I will attempt an answer.

I have written this book based on what I have learned and put to the test as a frequent public speaker and speaker coach myself. I have drawn upon lessons from a wide range of speakers I have heard, watched, analyzed, and tutored. This ability I owe to my own teachers and guides in communication, my dad, the Dale Carnegie instuctor, and my former boss, President Ronald Reagan, the Great Communicator.

CHAPTER ONE

Words Power the World

Launching a Competitive Message in a Crowded Marketplace

Imagine, for a moment, a round-the-clock cacophony of sound emanating from the packed streets of Manhattan, America's largest and most densely populated urban territory. It used to be that a city like New York slept at night. There was a cooling off and quieting down after midnight. Maybe people were sleeping, talking on their phones, relaxing, reading a book, finishing homework, having quiet conversations, or watching television. Whatever they were doing, there was more listening and a somewhat slower pace at night. It doesn't happen as much anymore.

There used to be neighborhoods where you could escape the noise. Now there is a permanent restlessness on almost every city block. Too many people in too few spaces, and it feels like they are all in motion—physically and mentally. Walking, biking, on scooters or skateboards. In one sense, the tension that arises from this physical proximity to the action is stimulating and, in another sense, it's stressful. Everywhere on the streets are sounds, almost like a muted Bruno Mars concert or the rappers Eminem or Tory Lanez all in the shadows and audible but mostly indiscernible and unrepeatable. Individual words might not be detected but the constant distant roar, the horns, and footsteps become the rhythm, cadence, and the beat of the symphony of a crowded city. Indeed, it's a lot like language!

Now, instead of people and their proximity in a city like New York, imagine the crowded world of words and their collision with one another in some type of frenzied, incoherent transmission. So many words are spoken and broadcast on expanding and multiplying platforms today that we risk being drowned in the traffic while possibly missing the meaning altogether. To compete in this crowded word-metropolis by delivering or broadcasting a speech or making a sales pitch is increasingly challenging.

While speech-giving has never been easy for most people, finding a pathway to make your voice heard in such a competitive environment in person, or over so many web-based platforms, has become an even greater challenge. Imagine the thousands of speeches, talks, messages being delivered every single hour of every day around the globe. Persuasion and storytelling—and the words that make this happen—power the world. Schools, universities, community centers, hotel conference rooms, stadiums, concert halls, government and political forums, web-based platforms—all are alight with words in front of both live and remote audiences.

In the realm of verbal communication, it is estimated that women speak an average of 20,000 words a day and men 7,000.

Between them there is a lot of talking, recording, performance, meetings, writing, speeches, broadcasting, all pushed out in vast quantities unimagined only a few years ago. Will we ever reach a saturation point at which time audiences stop considering certain issues because the marketplace in words has flooded the imagination? In fact even the security and safety of words have been compromised to affect acts of aggression and manipulation. Will this make us reticent to send more words out into an insecure environment, uncertain about how they might be franchised and manipulated?

Observers also sound alarms about the possibly excessive amount of information pouring out in front of audiences in relation to what they feel are requisite pauses required for deeper analysis, meditation, and contemplation, especially of profound or complex technical, educational, or even artistic material. It is difficult to know what would arrest this ultra-advancing trend, when more and more content is available, delivery more urgent and competitive, and the symphony of word-sounds is more difficult to penetrate. This makes a marketplace for any public speaker, business or government, and their content, more dense and challenging.

It is tough, for sure, to be an effective messenger and have your voice heard in such a complex market and at a time when audiences are becoming less apt to listen to a live presentation. It is more convenient to explore information pulsed on social media and available at all hours and in all settings. Add this to an audience more accustomed to processing data than contemplating ideas, and it is a steep hill to climb. This is a very serious issue for culture and human progress in general. Rapid advancement in the use of artifical intelligence or AI will complicate the deployment and analysis of information and word messages sent through impersonal machine messengers.

It is this disruptive word-climate that gave rise, in part, to the Trump style of speaking, one that he honed at the real estate negotiating table and the *Apprentice* reality television show. It was unconventional by political and governmental standards, but was reflective of a high-stakes win-or-lose proposition at the business bargaining table. It reinforces the principle grounded in ancient Greek culture that all public speaking is selling and persuading.

Do Words Always Deliver Their Intended Meaning?

The widely accepted standard bearer of word definitions and derivations, the *Oxford English Dictionary*, contains 171,476 words and adds approximately 1,000 new words every year. On average, however, today an individual English language speaker uses only 3,000, or approximately two-tenths of 1 percent, of these words in writing or speaking. But words by themselves are one-dimensional and inert until they are spoken, written, exclaimed, or sung—and placed in a context along with other words. Thus joined, they become messages or missiles that can have impact, be educational, or even result in disruption or consolation. Words well chosen and paired with effective delivery can form a compelling compact resulting in meaning and enlightenment; anger and threats; entreaties, proposals, and deals; as well as explanation, instruction, and inspiration—just to mention a few intentions from words well placed in relation to the listening ear and discerning mind.

Words can be used, intentionally or unintentionally, to manipulate, control, and mislead an audience as well as to inform, inspire, or entertain. Words alone can change the outcome of a court case, land a person in jail, make a marriage proposal or lose one, establish a friendship or end it, raise or lower the equity value of a company, result in a job or be fired from one. Words and delivery can be hurtful or helpful, powerful or pitiful. But words must be heard and intellectually or emotionally processed to acquire meaning and import. When offered ineffectively, even words that flow from the heart, mind, and mouth of the speaker might not be received in a way that the words are meant to be heard. What remains from the transmission of words, in terms of value or impact, is how the hearer processes them. Without that delivery of meaning to the listener's mind, why make the speech in the first place?

Alf Rehn, a popular writer and professor from Finland, has retold a poignant story in his article "The Art of Keynoting" about how what is said may not be what is heard. This is illustrated by what happened one day after he delivered a keynote speech.

> *I felt it had worked rather well, and the CEO was very appreciative. I hung around afterwards, listened to a few other speeches, and then joined in the lunch buffet. As I was walking around with my plate of salad and various meats, I walked straight into a heated argument. Two men, who both worked at the host company, were already raising their voices at each other. It seemed they had very different opinions regarding the key way to make an organization more creative, and in*

addition they both agreed that I was right about this. Both had heard the exact same speech but came away with diametrically opposed ideas regarding the central problem, and were now quite thrilled to see me, as both assumed that I would side with them. With a sense of dread, I asked both to recap their core take-away, which they did, placing me in the somewhat awkward position of having to tell both of them that they'd (both) misunderstood what I was trying to say.

This seems like a relatively harmless, yet possibly costly, lack of accurate message transmission; but the stakes, in political and especially multicultural, multilateral organizations and negotiations can be downright dangerous. More than that, these misunderstandings can appear in our conversations at work (as in this story) and at home and among families as an everyday occurrence.

As an example of what is spoken by one person that may not be heard in the same context by the listener, I have my own potent memory from a high-stakes encounter. It comes from my negotiations with Chinese officials on behalf of the US government. Every position we articulated and every request we made of our Chinese counterparts at the bargaining table in central Beijing was met with an emphatic "No!" This continued over many days and in lengthy and tedious meetings. We began to wonder if they even heard what we were asking for. We also wondered if their "no" actually meant "maybe" or even "yes." We learned that in some Asian cultures people may not react well to requirements for face-to-face acceptance or denial in a negotiation. They may prefer to deliver their real answers in sealed letters or impersonal documents, quite literally "saving face."

And that is precisely what we experienced in the Chinese capital.

Tired and tested by repeatedly long days of unsuccessful talks and a steady diet of exotic foods like monkey brains and sea slugs, we left the bargaining table in the State Guest House and climbed aboard an official US Air Force plane and flew back to Washington. Prepared to accept defeat from our efforts, we were pleasantly surprised to find our Chinese counterparts had acquiesced to all our demands—*after we left!* They delivered their acceptance in writing to the Secretariat of the National Security Council which announced the about-face as soon as our team was all assembled in the fabled Situation Room in the basement of the West Wing.

Pride had figured largely in their ancient communication protocol, and by our physically leaving the bargaining table, as we did, it gave them a safe way to accommodate us formally in writing—while maintaining their pride.

Westerners tend to be more direct, impatient, and demanding in their face-to-face negotiating styles. It is critical for any negotiator or speaker to learn these cultural distinctions in the way words are conveyed, understood, and, most critically, acted upon. You don't have to be negotiating with a foreign power to risk creating a gap between what is said and what is heard. This may be like telling a child to stop speaking with a mouthful of food and they keep right on doing it! They might interpret your command as meaning to "someday" stop talking with a mouth full of food. Your perception of what a person with whom you are speaking is hearing—and what that person believes you are saying—will always be just that. Your only test of validity is if the other party takes action as a direct result of what you have asked of them.

Transferring information from one human mind to another requires the passage of words, either in writing or speaking. This transfer may be precise or imperfect, and the initiator may not ever know how the message is actually received. Teachers may be in a unique position to discover the degree to which their lecture content reaches their targeted goal by requiring students to take a quiz or write an essay afterward. This usually determines to what degree the message migrated from the teacher to the students. For politicians, pollsters typically measure the degree to which campaign or policy messaging reaches the voting population. Ultimately, the success of the messaging is measured at the ballot box. To be judged effective, the speaker's message has to not only reach the ear of his listener but also his mind, his consciousness—and then, most importantly, affect his action at the ballot box.

After every Reagan speech, our pollsters were busy tallying the rise and fall of the president's public confidence polling numbers. Did the speech do its job? Did his speech resonate and reach the targeted audience? In a White House like Reagan's that revolved around communication, poll numbers were like fuel—to just about all of us, but with one big exception: President Reagan himself.

Reagan understood that in any polling, the critical question is who is doing the polling and who is doing the interpreting. Are they influenced by people with an interest in what people should think of what is said? Are polling answers affected by the ways questions are asked? Does whether or not the sun shines that day affect polling results? And what about the slice of the population

Reagan was known as the Great Communicator in part because of his authentic character and sincerity.

that happens to be in the polling audience—is it properly representative? As scientific and sophisticated as polling has become, these potential variables may have been part of why Reagan paid little attention to polls, always questioning their reliability and susceptibility to manipulation and interpretation.

The Evolving Use of Words and Their Impact on Culture

Any person who has a phone or an individual communication device can become a broadcaster of their own ideas ranging from the truly inspirational to the mundane or manipulating and disturbing. And those ideas can be conveyed with a fervor ranging from the mild and acceptable to malicious intent. Each person can be his own network to broadcast information—with few restrictions. Becoming an influencer and monetizing your own beliefs, styles, opinions has been a successful strategy for thousands who have found a way to build large groups of followers willing to take their advice or mimic their lifestyle and make purchases as a result. That is why commercial networks and storefronts are increasingly challenged and strained for ways to earn revenue from the traditional channels of communication and advertising paid for by retail advertisers in the past.

Today the generally accepted view is that all information and all media platforms that deliver it should be free and accessible globally. Access to content and media and the ability to create and broadcast it are seen, increasingly, to be a universal right. Ownership of data and content is a massive issue and will increasingly affect the delivery of information and messaging. These factors create additional challenges to public speakers and, it seems, the speaking industry, and have already produced an effect on how speakers are compensated.

Facing fierce criticism about their political platforms and assertive styles of delivery, both Reagan and Trump were forced to take control of their own messages and their deployment to their audiences. Both pioneered and ushered in new devices, platforms, and pathways for an American head of state to communicate directly with his constituents—thus avoiding the uncontrollable filter of the media. This practice is becoming increasingly commonplace and will grow in the future.

Both Reagan and Trump clearly recognized their need to speak directly to their audiences, without going through interpreting journalists or social media platforms. It worked and paid significant dividends, more or less, for both leaders while weakening the platforms of some journalists and traditional conveyers of the "news." During both presidential administrations overall public approval of the media dipped significantly and has landed today at an approximate level slightly below the public approval rating for the US Congress.

While Reagan stayed far away from direct confrontation with the media, Trump has taken a direct and assertively hostile approach to them. For both of these presidents the prospect of any conservative president who could command more generally positive views from journalists seemed an unrealizable dream since, even according to a survey of companies and CEOs covered by *Investor's Business Daily*, 95 percent of all financial reporters identify as left-of-center or politically moderate. Aside from these dueling positions, both a respected media as well as a respected Congress are fixtures critical to an effectively functioning democracy. We need a higher level of public confidence in both.

Reagan had his own discipline for a controlled and focused messaging strategy, designed to reach his listeners directly. He invented a Theme for the Day Team, on which I had the privilege of serving. He also started his own weekly radio show, creating and employing a platform for unfiltered delivery. Reagan spoke on radio every Saturday morning to a global audience, while Trump tweets sometimes hourly, seven days a week. His preferred platform of Twitter is largely novel for a head of state, although first used by President Obama. Reagan's radio platform was more conventional. In addition, his press secretary briefed the media daily, and the president himself spoke directly to the American people more frequently from the Oval Office than almost any other president. Reagan's communication team was larger than that of any of his predecessors. The stage management of Reagan's speeches was extensive, intricate, precise, ambitious.

In business, successful messaging and the deployment of words depends upon how they are selected, parsed, conveyed, emphasized, and even graphically depicted. Advertising agencies use key words and pictures to subconsciously manipulate thought and compel people to listen and take action in the marketplace. They may even cleverly hide these words in ways that they become graphically suggestive without the consumer even being aware of having seen the words or word-pictures.

Sports coaches know the right phrases and vocal timbre to stimulate a team to do better as well as the best way to shout or signal to get a result on the playing field. Singers may sympathetically change the mood from passive to romantic or the reverse. Parents may learn the best words and tone to compel their children to complete their homework, eat their dinner, or go to bed. Words are currency traded and employed in life's scenarios. Words have thoughts behind them. These transactions might take place in an intimate setting between two people or in a stadium of thousands.

A fundamental rule in all public speaking is to be aware of how your words will be received by your audience. To be ignorant of the possible impact of what you say is not a legitimate defense of the possible outcome. The speaker must take responsibility for the results. Inattentiveness and ignorance in this category can be costly. Although it is commonplace today to lob unvetted and possibly unfactual statements at an audience, they ultimately detract from the speaker's credibility.

The assertive use of language to manipulate the audience either for personal, business, or political purposes and outcomes is more commonplace today than in the past fifty years of modern communication. It is hard to imagine a reverse in this growing trend. The inevitable result may be greater disparity between what is said and what is heard—pointing to a greater responsibility on the part of the speaker to use metaphors, illustration, instruction, and repetition to gain an honest and accurate desired result. More speech givers need to carefully assess how their words and delivery will be received, or they may be misunderstood in ways that could diminish their credibility or cause harm and disruption to the organizations they represent.

Culturally this is an important topic, in part because a higher level of coarseness in language and the lessening of moderation in the deployment of words has risen, while self-restraint and self-knowledge have receded—all in the wildly competitive drive to influence and manipulate others with exciting and possibly disruptive text. There are thousands of highly paid influencers in the marketplace competing with any individual just seeking to share information without monetary gain. The media platforms and networks that host 24/7 commentary have increased, and the intense competition for advertisers has increased as well. Since for most media outlets income is generated from sponsors or advertisers who require a minimum number of "hits" from readers or listeners, they often promote controversy—imagined or genuine—to draw attention to their content and to what they are selling.

The current trajectory of public communication does not lead us to believe that the traditional formalities of dignity and civility will again soon predominate in all the heated halls of discourse and debate. While many speeches still adhere to a modest standard of civility and politeness, look for more talks to display less pleasant discursiveness and more directness reflective of everyday communication patterns. To some extent language used in speeches is reflective of the general cultural discourse and always has been—even though a higher level of language, tone, and usage in oratory has traditionally been followed. These are the speeches that inform and interpret culture and have largely endured through the ages. The future portends a veering off this course.

CHAPTER TWO

Words and Images: The Fuel of Persuasion

The Laws of Persuasion

Public oratory originated in ancient Greece and was notably promoted and taught by Aristotle and Plato, who engineered the rules of rhetoric. They developed them in part from necessity as the political evolution in that Mediterranean crucible evolved. They defined rhetoric as the art of persuasion. Rhetoric was not only critical to these teachers and philosophers but equally essential to the growing political debate in which, for the first time, ordinary citizens participated in and sustained new forms of government. Their students ushered in and demonstrated some of the most basic and fundamental elements of modern society based on public conversations, discourse, and debate, as well as full-blown oratorical speeches. In fact, the first leader of the Greek democracy, Pericles, was not called a president or prime minister; he was named a citizen leader, selected for his very ability to persuade. He was referenced as

the "Chief Persuader." Highly skilled persuasion was needed
to help unite this string of independent city-states joining
together for the first time in a united front against agitators
and antagonistic invaders and aggressors. Persuasion became
their vital defense.

You might say that the art of persuasion, in addition to
skilled military maneuvers, brought these factions and various dialects together to form what we call ancient Greece.
While we admire the various architectural types of fabled
Greek columns on the Athenian temples that hosted these
debates, the burgeoning pillars of democracy were quite literally being developed and supported by a growing skill in public speaking. These oratorical skills were not a luxury practiced
by the few. They were an outright necessity for all citizens as
the foundation of a free and responsible society. Their growth
was essential for the expansion of participatory democracy as it
took shape and foretold a dynamic future.

For a progressive and learned democracy, delivering oratory freely without constraint and yet subject to debate in the
public square was an ideal birthed in the Athenian cradle of
democracy. It has always been critical to foundational precepts
wherever democracy has flourished in succeeding centuries. In
fact, the development of citizen speaking skills remains absolutely essential to participatory government today and is one of
the guardians of freedom. The early Greek thinker, Socrates
wrote: "There is no institution devised by man which the
power of speech has not helped to establish."

This rhetorical ability was a newfound and essential part
of democracy. Before this, ordinary citizens were not generally regarded for their opinions, so there was little necessity

Aristotle was one of the inventors of and first teachers of rhetoric on which the Greek democracy was dependent.

for dramatic and successful oratory. Storytelling provided the principal strands of communication and historical recordkeeping and its skill was woven into the fabric of ancient families, communities, and cultures.

In the fifth century BC, Plato further defined rhetoric with five canons or laws, which included Invention, Arrangement, Elocution, Memory, Delivery. Thousands of years later, these basic tenets remain at the core of our own effective speech training. Just as it was in Greece, public speaking was also considered a right and a responsibility of Roman citizenship. Hundreds of years after Plato introduced his canons, to speak in the Roman public forum deploying the refined art of the orator became a prized accomplishment. Cicero, a Roman senator, even founded a school for communication and declared Roman oratory fundamentally important to the rule of the empire. The Roman citizen Corax became the first professional speech coach to charge for his services. This led to an entire industry of professionals in the burgeoning coaching field.

There was another reason rhetorical training was so important to the Romans. As ownership and property rights grew with democratic rule and prosperity, people were required to represent themselves in the courts since, in the early days of the empire, there were no professional lawyers to do this for them. Imagine life without lawyers today, where every man or woman has to speak eloquently and effectively enough on their own behalf to win a court case, transfer property rights, or keep themselves out of jail. There would be a surge of people attending public speaking schools, and masterful oratory would be more commonplace.

Don't imagine, however, that the discussions, speeches, and

debates of Greece and Rome were exclusively high-minded. Speeches could even lead to beheadings and often carried a high cost in a political field where there could be heated argument and disagreement—not unlike today, although, thankfully, we do not have the physical brutality of the ancient Greeks and Romans. Still, the contemporary coarseness of high-stakes political discourse we hear now is a byproduct of speaking in the public square more than two thousand years ago.

The American founders were also active debaters and had fierce disagreements. But they expressed disapproval of their peers less often in direct talking and more often in private letters. Thomas Jefferson, for example, had a famous feud with John Adams for many years as evidenced in scorching letters that continued until they agreed on a truce, finally remaining friends and friendly correspondents expressed in 1,400 letters over fourteen years before both died on the same day on America's birthday, July 4, 1826. Open debate, however, was commonplace, necessary, and plentiful as the Constitutional delegates tested divergent approaches to the many details of a wholly new form of government.

For example, strong arguments were voiced among the delegates at the Constitutional Convention on the precise job description for a chief executive—one that would not replicate the British monarchy they had rejected and fled. There were also disagreements on how this new leader would be elected. There were hundreds of issues to debate, ranging from the idealistic to the practical, and there were almost as many individual opinions as delegates. It is, however, breathtaking to imagine the texture, delivery, and content of these fervent orations and their gravity because, after all, they were forming a wholly new approach to government based on the opposite of what they had suffered under and escaped from. No doubt they felt the weight of responsibility and the great risks to their fellow citizens if they failed to form a workable and lasting compact.

The very fact that they could openly debate, and sometimes even lose a proposition on the architecture of this new government, is an object example of the necessity and durability of effective oration. Among the many subjects that earned their complete agreement was the fundamental protection of freedom of speech as expressed in the First Amendment to the Constitution, and by this action sanctioning and furthering the role of unfettered oration and its undeniable component in protecting a free and open society.

Just as classical rules of rhetoric and discourse were prized and put to use by the American founders who sponsored open and sometimes raucous debates among the delegates to the Continental Congress, it is in this tradition that a liberal education, especially in democratic societies, has often included training in elocution, rhetoric, and oratory.

Thomas Jefferson insisted on incorporating this curriculum and pedagogy when he created his classical University of Virginia. Today, speech classes focus less on the rules of traditional oratory and more on pragmatic topics such as selling and job seeking and are typically required at community colleges and also at some four-year liberal arts institutions. These types of offerings are strangely missing from many business school courses of instruction. Perhaps this lack of training contributes to so many unforced and expensive errors on the part of corporate communicators.

Although the art of speaking was considered among his

Thomas Jefferson did not like the softness of his voice, nevertheless his voice was heard through great speakers who invoked his thoughts and words for him.

significant accomplishments, Jefferson himself did not consider his oratorical skills to be sufficiently successful because of his soft-spoken voice. This may be one reason he focused on a prolific writing career, which more than made up for his lack of oratorical acuity. His learned writing was drawn from his expansive reading of the classics, his fertile analytics and wide-ranging curiosity, and from his experiences as an envoy for his young country in Europe. Jefferson used the classical string of three nouns to move his prose, as in his Declaration of Independence, which included in its second paragraph: "We hold these truths to be self-evident, that all men are created equal and they are endowed by their Creator with certain unalienable Rights, that among these are Life, Liberty and the pursuit of Happiness."

What Jefferson may have personally thought he lacked in speaking ability has been compensated by the many truly effective speakers who have used his words for content in thousands of speeches. I could never forget one remarkable evening attending a candlelit dinner at Monticello, Jefferson's remarkable Charlottesville home, listening to Prime Minister Margaret Thatcher recite Jefferson in her acceptance of the first Jefferson Medal for Diplomacy, which I had helped to establish. In this case the formidable prime minister was not just reading Jefferson's words and citing his outsize scientific and diplomatic accomplishments, while comparing them to hers, she was adopting his meaning and eloquently expressing it to an impressive crowd of national leaders. She was using her voice to speak Jefferson's rhetoric.

While you may not be a member of the US Congress or even hold a public position that requires regular high-stakes speech-making, you may decide to become a fluent, proficient

Margaret Thatcher told me that at times she was fearful of public speaking so she would talk herself out of her fear, forge ahead, and prevail.

rhetorical speaker as a teacher or to advance your career, to become more active in community or political affairs, or to grow personally. You may be required to do so as a part of your job description in business, such as a salesperson, CEO, or head of investor relations. Very few of us are natural, native-born public speakers. We learn to speak, more or less, by age three. But these are basic verbal skills needed to function and fulfill basic needs. Outside of these life skills, to communicate on behalf of a company, a cause, or crusade might be optional or inspirational, or it may be simply required of you.

You may also have spent years hiding from these responsibilities or thwarting opportunities to speak, and you may have finally reached the point where this strategy of avoidance will not work. Some people join public speaking groups, such as Toastmasters, without a professional aim or ambition, but for self-improvement and growth in self-confidence and interpersonal relations. The most practical first step is to ask yourself why you seek to speak effectively in public and what you hope to accomplish by honing your skills. The answer to this question will point you to the proper training and practice you need to accomplish your goal. Complete honesty and candor in assessing your skills are essential to acquiring a sufficient degree of self-knowledge that is the first step in developing these skills.

Words and Images Are Partners in Persuasion

When I joined the Reagan team in 1981, I had to learn the power of persuasion in a political context. I had to learn a film-industry approach to the presidency that included sophisticated site advance work, staging, lighting, makeup, wardrobe, sound, backdrops, scenery, projection, audience development—all aspects that were commonplace to the Reagans. I also had to learn about the phenomenal tricks of the trade for the highly skilled Reagan White House advance teams. I didn't even know what an advance man was when I stepped into the West Wing. For any speech that had a particular theme, the advance office required the perfect visual backdrop to support, elevate, and dramatize the words being spoken. They knew that photographic and film images are powerful tools of persuasion and are partners with the impact of the spoken word.

In no place was this more evident than on foreign state visits. These photo ops became the stock-in-trade of our creative advance office working together with the speechwriters. Together, our goal was always to show interest in the host country and to foster good bilateral policy through verbal as well as nonverbal pictorial communication. To achieve this, our advance office, as in any presidential administration, worked in tandem with the advance teams representing major media outlets whose goal was the same as ours: to capture the dramatic picture and to be well positioned to achieve it in a way that it might become an exclusive. After all, their publications depended on the art of photography, film, and photojournalism to sell copies.

For Reagan to have given the Berlin Wall speech from a nearby stadium or a hotel ballroom in downtown Berlin would never have achieved the dramatic historic impact of seeing Reagan standing in front of the contentious, graffiti-covered barrier that denied a country its freedom and reunification. Making the picture in Berlin more poignant were the East

Berlin security forces standing with their rifles poised for attack and focused on the presidential party. The White House advance team could not have asked for anything more effective. It was political theater at its finest.

Likewise, in Moscow, when the Reagans took their highly choreographed and widely televised stroll in Red Square in front of Lenin's tomb, or made their quick "unplanned" walk down Arbat Street, the message was sharper than any formal speech in a hotel conference room. Both Reagan and Trump visited the DMZ in Korea. Trump actually stepped into the North. Reagan remained in the Zone, wearing a telegenic green army parka with a fur-trimmed hood. Both photos gained widespread attention and sent timely messages to the rest of the world. Photos from foreign trips and speeches in unusual places are sure to gain respectability and widespread coverage for a president.

The Reagans were roundly criticized by the press for spending too much time with royalty as recorded in many photographs promoting their relationship. Trump gained some stature by his state visit to England and his welcome by the royal family. These are examples of the effectiveness of nonverbal communication to sell a person or an idea. In these cases, of course, the photo opportunity has to be partnered with an effective speech or graceful comments. Otherwise the goodwill accomplished by the photo could work in the opposite, possibly disastrous, direction. Such was the case when Reagan visited the Bergen-Belsen cemetery where Holocaust victims were buried along with members of the German SS. The photo ops were brief and rushed, and Reagan's remarks logically focused on the victims who lay at rest there and not their persecutors. By insisting on abiding by his commitment to German Chancellor Kohl to make this stop, despite being advised not to go, Reagan withstood controversy at home. Reagan could be just as unmovable in his views and beliefs and as unyielding to the pleas of his spouse and advisers as Trump, and this was one example of it.

In Reagan's presidency, communication was as important as policy, and it brought results. This was the direct opposite of Reagan's predecessor Jimmy Carter, who keenly valued and coyly manipulated his media coverage—but not always to his advantage—as revealed in hindsight. Carter longed to be portrayed by the media as the authentic and caring average Joe, but the way he managed his everyday media image did not help him in these categories of nonverbal communication. For example, although Reagan barely, if ever, mentioned his own faith in a personal way, people believed he was a deeply committed Christian. Carter mentioned his faith repeatedly, and yet it was not a help for him when his election for a second term came around.

Trump, overturning tradition, as he has in many aspects of presidential leadership, has become his own press secretary. My friend Jay Nordlinger, writing about presidential communication in the *National Review*, said that "Style matters, and it may matter more than the policy," and both Reagan and Trump exhibited unique styles, as did John F. Kennedy, who was heralded for creating the first truly ready-for-prime-time television presidency. Style in communicating is a brand builder that both Reagan and Trump focused on successfully. It won them sustained legacies resulting from how and where they spoke more than, in some cases, what they said.

President Kennedy launched the first truly telegenic presidency where speeches were seen and not just heard. He became a master at presentation as well as content, laying down the gauntlet for the standard in communication and production for all his successors.

Dilbert cartoonist Scott Adams, who has labeled Trump the Master Persuader, has assessed the Trump phenomenon in his successful book *Win Bigly*. He has posited that Trump's sometimes imprecise statements or factual inaccuracies have not hurt him, in the eyes of his supporters, at all. Adams says:

> *If you ever tried to talk someone out of their political beliefs by providing facts, you know it doesn't work. That's because people think they have their own facts. Better facts...And facts are weak persuasion...So Trump ignores facts whenever they are inconvenient.*

Furthermore, Adams goes on to advise any speaker this way: "A good general rule is that people are more influenced by visual persuasion, emotion, repetition, and simplicity than they are by details and facts." He also says that Trump uses "solid gold visual persuasion" and advises, "If you are using super strong persuasion, you can be wrong on the facts, and even the logic of your argument, and still win."

While Adams does accurately and interestingly describe the Trump formula for success, for the rest of us mere mortals I am not sure I would fully endorse the Adams point of view about factual accuracy. At a minimum I would not encourage any public speaker to throw out the vetting process when it comes to delivering the facts. Politicians may have the luxury of massive stage productions and distracting poster-waving to create a visual experience that competes with facts and diverts attention, but most speakers do not have these devices at hand. One factual misstep can send a speaker right off the list of possible performers for future events.

Persuasive words and messages today are propelled by massive social media platforms that host written and spoken words and broadcast them to billions across the globe. Once these words are unleashed on social media platforms, like the adage about the toothpaste never being put back into the tube, they typically cannot be completely retrieved and expunged. An amendment or correction to or censoring of words broadcast on social media, if found necessary, often reinforces the original mistake and stirs even more controversy rather than erasing or limiting the impact or damage.

An example of this was in the memorable and costly lapse of judgment when Tony Hayward, CEO of British Petroleum, after spending a few days examining the extent of the damage from the massive 2010 Gulf of Mexico oil spill, bemoaned his lack of personal time to get back to the UK and go yachting on his own boat. He notoriously said, in the wake of eleven deaths on their oil rig, that he wanted "my life back." No manner of apology can ever erase that from the minds of those who heard him state his preference for personal recreation over managing an oil spill that did untold damage to the environment, families, and to jobs. Hayward paid the price and lost his job, but the story has had a long shelf life. Hayward did a poor job of attempting to persuade the public and regulators that BP was a responsible energy company. They recently announced a total retreat from North America.

Using Digital Platforms to Deliver Persuasion

Today social media platforms are like jet propulsion labs that enable words to reach around the globe to connect listeners to them synchronously and asynchronously. To illustrate not only how pervasive and powerful these sites are, look at the release of financial data from major corporations and government institutions on a minute-by-minute basis on Facebook, Twitter, Instagram, LinkedIn, or YouTube. The demand is for transparency and for ubiquitous data to be delivered at light speed and disseminated by the sender in real time. This will be even more potent when 5G is universally adopted.

Today analysts are always waiting for fresh data around the clock, whether sitting at CIA station desks or at Goldman Sachs trading monitors. What looms large now is alarm over the security of personal and corporate information and the manipulation of voice tones or facial recognition. It is a massive security concern with major global ramifications, including cyber warfare which is already underway. If your words and what you say can be manipulated by your adversary or a cyber thief and extortionist for their own purposes, the veracity of every single statement broadcast using social media platforms might become suspect and the whole global transmission of data cast into doubt. Financial data and political campaigns are the obvious and most highly threatened because on them hinge both our future global and individual personal security.

Former US Secretary of Defense Caspar Weinberger forecast this in his prescient and riveting 1996 book about cyber warfare titled *The Next War*. This prediction has come true. Cyber war is already here. The impact of the massive 2017 Equifax data security breech that affected 147 million people hasn't even begun to be felt because the data are still being held by the perpetrators. Whoever controls words and data, as well as their transmission platforms, controls the world.

Approximately 50 percent of the world's population of around 7.8 billion people participate in social media in some way, and the numbers are growing. Two billion people use YouTube alone, watching a total of five billion videos a day. The traffic in words has reached a fever pitch. Many people go to bed reading messages on their phones even while attempting to solve problems that arise from a widespread lack of sleep and resulting chronic health issues.

My friend Arianna Huffington, herself an early developer, promoter, and exploiter of the digital revolution, has turned to promoting effective sleep as essential to health and well-being. The obsession with social media has also resulted in a lowering of the average human attention span to between a minimum of fifteen seconds to a maximum of eight minutes, minimizing tolerance for true and accurate listening and more thoughtful and analytical processing of content. This phenomenon affects, in a major way, how we prepare for and deliver speeches.

The meaning of words and their comprehension by the speaker also affects how audiences hear and focus their attention span and how they digest the message and their memory of it. These are all points the public speaker must bear in mind when preparing a talk. Awareness of these features is critical to forming your principal message and understanding your targeted listeners and how they might respond or react to your message. This is why we are discussing the environment for the spoken word.

Speeches today do not employ the precise vocabulary or word construction of even a decade ago. Language and usage have evolved and are significantly affected by the lexicon of technology. Colloquialisms come and go, and reference points, stories, and jokes that do not reflect the lives we now live may fail to persuade and sell because they have outlived their usefulness in speeches and should be retired from use entirely. However, to abandon the record of the past may be dangerous to our future and to our lives, communities, and society in general. It was Churchill who advised prophetically, "The farther you can look back, the further you can go into the future."

Reagan, of course, drenched his speeches in references to the past, employing, in 96 percent of his speeches, quotations from and references to great leaders, patriots, prophets, and presidents of both parties. This gave his speeches more of a universality and commonality and made what he said less personal and more generic to the proven wisdom of greater minds than his—or so he made you think, as a listener.

All Politics Is Persuasion

Political scientist and writer Richard Neustadt commented that "Presidential power is the power to persuade." By this definition Trump is a gladiator. An ultra-competitor. This is fascinating because even while he professes not to talk about policy, he creates it by bringing his audience along with him on an oratorical roller-coaster. Doing this garners enough support to sponsor his outsize accomplishments in the economy, trade, tax reform, and foreign policy—and to stir up an equal share of political opposition and controversy as well as anger, feigned and real, from his opponents.

In contrast to Reagan, Trump rarely references the past

or specific quotations from leaders of the past, even though his political platform is based on traditional American values. Trump himself interprets and gauges what his audiences want to hear. His messages are all about today and today's problems and solutions. They are comprised of more action and impact-oriented language than philosophical or historical word choices that would seem inauthentic to him. After all, there is nothing more ineffective than a speaker mouthing the words, thoughts, and beliefs of other people that do not truly reflect his own. Trump's language is simple, explosive, and direct. He returns frequently to words he is sure of, and his audiences follow right along. The simple construction of his sentences and the repetition of his claims and word choice fit nicely with the people who agree with his views, and there are millions who do. Those attending his speeches or rallies do not clamor for more sophisticated speeches.

Reagan and his speechwriters felt much of the great writing and orations of the past are important to repeat in speeches, not only for their content but also for their structure, richness, symmetry, and substance. The record of the past was all-important to Reagan because he felt it might arm us against possible repeated and egregious mistakes that could be avoided by considering and adhering to the wisdom contained in these recitations of the past.

Today a successful public speaker might pair evolving contemporary word choices and their meanings with what are generally considered wise orations of the past to reinforce the rhetoric of new speeches. Reagan almost always did this in every speech he made. He used the past as metaphor to guide the future. In this way he was drawing guidance from the past as it might affect the present and the future. This was a brilliant tactic and one that Reagan even joked about in self-deprecation, referring to his advanced age as president, when he would say, "And remember, I know Thomas Jefferson felt that way, because I *knew* Thomas Jefferson."

Trump, however, enters the ring at a time when history and the past are barely visible and more rarely employed oratorically or practically in developing or communicating policy. Contemporary airtime is so filled with new views, opinions, attitudes, and disruption that there is hardly room for the historical perspective. Of course, this can be dangerous, and we see the results in uninformed, uneducated discourse and lack of appreciation for historical records and knowledge. In public speaking now, the present and the future are the major features of Trump time—not historic considerations. Trump is the "barker" or ringmaster in what sometimes feels like a very current carnival of politics.

Web-based Platforms Power Persuasion

For performance and persuasive powers, TED talks, TEDx, MasterClass, YouTube, Instagram, web-based video instruction and advertising, webinars, podcasts, and other iterative talking and persuading formats have set a standard and have been massively influential in style and substance in their attempt to cut through a crowded space and focus the audience mostly on the remarkable and listenable stories of champions and the discoveries of innovative thinkers and doers. TED talks require their speakers to focus on one major idea of current importance, give people a reason to care about the idea, build the idea with familiar concepts, and, finally, make the idea worth sharing or, in other words, prove its impact. These condensed and compact presentations on topics of import delivered with personal stories and drama added in the mix have, in some ways, become the gold standard of speech giving, although they may have stylistically peaked in their influence.

One of the most watched TED talks is instructive, with more than 17.5 million views, which is Sir Ken Robinson's talk titled "Do Schools Kill Creativity?" I found it interesting that many people cited the principal reason he succeeds is his use of humor and humility mixed with starkly provocative opinions and novel thinking that strike a chord with the audience. It is one of those talks you send to your entire network with the heading "This is a must watch." Sir Ken weaves his own personal experience with his children into his message and is self-deprecating in a way that draws you to him and makes you want to believe all of his observations. This is persuasive storytelling at its best because it is purposeful and entertaining. And he is a performer, for sure. Very much like what every public speaker should wish to emulate as an example of effective delivery.

As a result of what Sir Ken said, I actually found myself wanting to join a crusade or his cause to move schools in the direction of adding more art, music, theater, and dance. He mobilized me because he was convincing. He uses facts and evidence to back up his claims. TED talks, viewed online but recorded before a live audience, also have the advantage of the energy and laughter of the appreciative in-person viewers. The laughter from the audience in the case of Sir Ken's talk adds luster and energy to his speech and makes you want to be one of the crowd applauding him as well. It's a potent formula, well vetted and watched and, I am sure, copied for its style.

Sir Ken is part of an enormous crowd of influencers and persuaders who have established YouTube channels to broadcast their messages. While it has proved a steep climb to monetize an average number of hits to a YouTube channel, there have been many who have been able to monetize hits to their content. YouTube wants more people to establish their own channels because they in turn then earn income from every hit.

We have been discussing words and their effective usage for speaking and broadcasting, for selling and persuasion, and having them heard by the listener in an intentional and targeted way. This affects our training and preparation as speakers and deliverers of messages in a time of growing and intense competition for a listening audience. The assumption is that if you put time and effort into crafting your message and find an audience to listen, you want to be heard, and you want to be informative, to educate, enlighten, effect change. You want your audience to buy something or to sign on to your declaration or opinion.

To be effective as speakers we need to know the competition and how to achieve a position in our listeners' minds that causes a change in consciousness. This requires building a bridge of credibility with the audience and then holding their attention with the energy, emotion, and vitality that can be conveyed by words—in some respects echoing the words of the book of Proverbs, "A word fitly spoken is like apples of gold in pictures of silver."

CHAPTER THREE

Discovering Your Authentic Self

Why Are You a Public Speaker?

We have discussed the busy world of words and how thousands of speeches, delivering millions of words, using all types of language and platforms, are underway in all parts of the world at any one time. And we have also talked about the persuasive power of words and discussed how platforms to deliver speeches are changing and sending messages into places previously unreachable by traditional routes. Of course, all these speeches are being given by people in all walks of life—each with a specific purpose.

How did we end up giving so many speeches, with so few of us trained to do so? In a sense it shows that despite the fact that approximately fifty countries in the world are ruled by dictators or suffer some form of significant limits on personal freedom, and freedom of speech, there is more talking, debating, and discussion going on around the globe than ever before in human history. This is all good. Ideally, unfettered, free, and uncoerced thinking and talking are essential to preserve self-determination, individual freedom, and open forms of limited government as well as free-market economies.

You may be called upon to speak for a purpose far from defending foreign policy as a US secretary of state, or as a university president addressing students and teachers. You may be managing a call center and speaking to customers all day long about their problems with technology or broken dishwashers. You might be a project manager training construction crews on safety practices. You might also be an online comic on your own YouTube channel. To excel at any one of these jobs requires an introspective self-examining dive, however shallow or deep, into a greater understanding of yourself.

Finding your authentic self and your success at public speaking are cause and effect. Understanding who you are in relation to a profession, performance, skill, or life experience can help turn you into an effective speaker. And this in turn will materially increase the level of your performance at any of these jobs, or as a platform speaker or salesperson, preacher or webinar educator. Your genuine authenticity is what will ultimately win your audience. Your content may be lacking, but if your customer believes in you, the sale is made. There is no more important rule to learn in public speaking as this.

How Recent Presidents Discovered Their Authenticity

As a teenager, Ronald Reagan sequestered himself from frequent family arguments in his own private space in the attics of the family's various rented houses. During these times he read novels and mysteries that helped him imagine he was living in a world distant from the dissonance below. His mother, Nelle, also required him to read the entire Bible, more than once, and memorize passages, and to perform in morality plays she would write or construct based on what he read. Nelle also gave him a novel to read on which he patterned his life. It included a protagonist with an alcoholic father, like Reagan's, who ended up in the halls of the US Capitol in Washington, as a congressman. For some people wrestling with significant family discord, the only route is isolation and insecurity but, to a large extent, Reagan conquered these tendencies.

He was a thespian in high school as well as a football lineman. The plays he acted in and his study of the Scriptures gave him content and beliefs he could speak about. By the time he was in college, he considered joining his best friend who was enrolling at Yale Divinity School after they graduated. As he explained it to me, he was encouraged in this direction by the father of the girl he intended to marry, Margaret Cleaver, who was the minister's daughter. This was the same minister who had also arranged a scholarship for him at the rural Illinois church school he attended, Eureka College.

By the time the future president had graduated from college he had developed confidence in his speaking ability and storytelling. So Reagan answered the first question I have asked all of you. Why do you want to be a speaker? What is your motivation? He had gained speaking skill, personal confidence, as well as a message, or content, based on his personal beliefs and a strong desire to conquer personal adversity. These were three key assets he had harnessed as he began to enter the world of public speaking. They also were excellent examples of gaining the self-knowledge and authenticity he would need.

But both Reagan and Trump also had the somewhat suppressed need to impress their demanding fathers and exceed their financial accomplishments. For Reagan, the logical next step into public speaking was largely motivated by economics. As he finished college, parted with Margaret, and decided against going into the ministry, he was offered a job as radio broadcast announcer for the Chicago Cubs baseball team. His extraordinary success, night after night, in creating verbal play-by-play narratives that made people think they were actually in the bleachers rather than listening on radio boosted his confidence in his speaking ability even higher. Now he knew he could win an audience.

When an opportunity developed to try out for films, he was prepared. He had a lot to say. He could talk fast, confidently, and had a high degree of self-knowledge, honed through mastering the adversity of having an alcoholic father who repeatedly disappointed him and gave him the need to conquer any tendency toward inwardness. The rest of the story for Reagan, the Great Communicator, is all found in a series of economic decisions made mostly out of financial insecurity and unemployment. He took the job as GE spokesperson because his film career was fading, the governorship because he needed a job and had sponsors and underwriters. In his final role, he ran for president largely because of his beliefs and less because of a salary, although his presidential campaigns and financial backers did provide a monetary supply for him and for his family while he was campaigning.

Reagan's story of a climb out of poverty and into a career of public speaking is not unlike the stories of many of us. It would be too idealized and not completely true to state that most people go into oratory because of a love of language. Churchill, the great orator, though born into wealth and position, had little of it bestowed on him so he wrote books because he needed the money that came from publishing. He lived his life mostly on the cusp of economic disaster and bankruptcy. That kept him talking, speech-giving, and ultimately writing forty books for a paycheck.

Our own time is filled with the stories of people who have made financial gain not only from publishing books but from public speaking. Tony Robbins, Arianna Huffington, Eckhart Tolle, Suze Orman, Jack Canfield, and Wayne Dyer are a few examples of people who built careers and financial success as public speakers. There are many more. For most people, though, public speaking can be a necessary but ancillary career or a scary requirement built into their job description.

Not completely unlike Reagan, although much less complex, Trump's developing ability to speak in public was steeped in economics as well. Trump was born, raised, and educated in the New York real estate marketplace where talking, communicating, winning, and developing the art of the deal were all woven into the fabric of his highly competitive personality. Trump monetized his ability to talk his way into a deal and out of one with outsize successes that fueled his public confidence, and with some failures that he refused to accept as limitation. He had selling and dealing in his DNA and brand-building as his business strategy.

Trump decided that to build an even more successful real estate firm than his dad's, he had to create a brand by which he could achieve a celebrity status. His success at brand-building

Trump has high energy typical of a man half his age and feeds his audience what they want to hear.

was completely dependent on his skill at winning an audience. In a sense he was a precursor of what we call influencers— people who build a massive group of followers on social media, and, in order to monetize their lifestyles, advertisers pay them to parade in and promote their goods and services. Trump was smart enough to become an early influencer. He understood one point of view in media relations: that all attention is good attention. All clicks are good clicks. All hits are good hits. It is a top-down sales approach to exposure. This is specifically what fuels his frenetic daily/hourly communication style and practice. There is a fear that if you let up on daily/hourly posting on social media, you will actually lose your audience. Ask any influencer and they will tell you that.

Trump was one of the first people to recognize, put to use, and manipulate social media in an ambitious way for his brand-building as he made money in real estate development. Once he jumped into the political arena, he was competing with a group of relative social media newcomers—at least compared to his years of aggressive personal brand-building. He left his competitors in the dust because he was willing to forge a new path as a national leader and not to follow some aspects of expected traditional presidential protocol. Because he was an unconventional person, he sold unconventionality with authenticity at a time when a significant disruption in communication, advertising, and selling was beginning to accelerate. His fiercest aim became to remain ahead of the pack. Trump was unwilling to take a back seat to anyone. This had appeal, on its own, to a majority of people who try to forge their own pathway every day on their own. Enough people admired his outspokenness, authenticity, and boldness.

Trump was an entrepreneur and, according to Babson College in 2018, he shared that title with twenty-five million self-proclaimed entrepreneurs and fifteen million self-employed people in the US. In this category of strivers, there is a high percentage of people who reliably cast votes for elected officials. Trump had a high percentage of these as a natural potential base because he was perceived as one of them. Many knew his story and had watched his television show *The Apprentice* and perhaps had seen his thirteen film cameos and eighteen television appearances in scripted shows. Although these media appearances could not compare to Reagan's film career of serious acting, Trump was not unfamiliar with lighting, scripts, and camera angles.

He also knew that 62 percent of American billionaires are self-made, and while not all billionaires supported him, he could make the claim that he crafted his financial success almost alone, and that had appeal to many for its directness and hubris. He utilized the same business and personal brand-building strategy to win the White House. The way he achieved his victory confirmed his authenticity, and he will not deviate from this formula. It is dependable, bankable, and as marketable in the political economy as it had been in real estate. There are those who are quickly trying to catch up to and use his playbook, but Trump will remain the first candidate to successfully gain the White House using his unique strategy.

In dramatically different ways, Reagan and Trump illustrate the essential element that leads to acceptance by any audience: authenticity. This may be the most difficult attribute to develop and adopt—though it is closest to your heart.

Self-knowledge is the key. It will keep you from speaking on a topic about which you know too little, using a vocal tone or phrasing in a way that is pretentious or not true to your natural voice—or even standing in a way that throws off or intimidates your audience.

You can stumble on the stairs on your way up to the podium, lose your place in your script, or become emotional, but if you are authentic to yourself—if you have the kind of self-knowledge that comes through even unspoken, you will win the day, despite your fumbling. Reagan and Trump are self-assured characters, but each audience they have won solidifies their unwavering commitment to a platform of ideals and strategies for winning again. The promises that each made were taken seriously by their audiences. It is on these promises that the bond with, and the bridges to, audiences have been built, and the barriers brought down.

How to Discover YOUR Authenticity

Why is being authentic the first and most critical step to complete acceptance by your audience, and what does being authentic mean? Any speaker can rise or fall in success even before their first word is spoken, because more than 50 percent of all communication is considered nonverbal. It is not just your physical appearance: your clothing, your makeup, your haircut, eye contact, or your posture—although these are important in *conveying* your authenticity. It is your state of thought, your acceptance of yourself, how you view and value yourself, and, most important, how you regard and value your audience and your message. It is what's going on inside of you that transports the inside of the listener—the individual waiting for your delivery.

Many scholars, psychologists, and teachers of oratory agree that conscious and nonconscious thinking, analysis, behavior, intention, focused thought can all be transferred from the speaker to the audience while speaking or not speaking. In 1971, Dr. Albert Mehrabian published *Silent Messages*, a book in which he asserted that a significant percentage of communication is nonverbal and this includes tone, feelings, inhibitions, mannerisms, eye contact, personal confidence and behavior, and unconscious thoughts. It is fascinating and also important to consider that the art of effective public speaking is really a mental or metaphysical as well as physical exercise. It is the sport of revealing orally, through sound, what is going on mentally in your conscious and subconscious mind.

Taking this approach helps explain the interrelationship between the verbal and nonverbal. It also leads us to understand why so many people are fearful of public speaking—an exercise that requires considerable personal exposure and vulnerability. An inauthentic speaker may be one who is closed off, invulnerable to and mentally inaccessible by the audience, since personal exposure may be too high a price to pay for them. As a result their behavior toward the audience might be seen as imperious or haughty to compensate for their lack of confidence. These costly insecurities may stem from any number of causes, usually having to do with upbringing or assumed insecurities or trauma left unresolved.

In a way, speaking in public is a revealing of the self and an exposure of self, which makes some people want to do anything but talk in front of others. Conversely, the opposite is true in many cases where speakers want to do nothing but talk about themselves. Note, however, that talking about oneself does not necessarily translate into being considered authentic or even confident, though it may come across that way initially. Excessive talking about oneself may be a mask or barrier to revealing truer aspects of the authentic self. *Talking about yourself does not equate to knowing yourself.* These factors figure in all speaking, even if your topic happens to be completely impersonal and scientific. It is still about your life and is a reflection of who you are and why and how you conducted the research that gives you credibility.

Now you might think, "Hey, I thought I was reading a book about how to be an effective public speaker, not a book on personal psychology!" And I am telling you that your complete success as a speaker is dependent on your conquering this one critical psychological point. So let's delve into it a bit more and try to figure this out together.

But first let me share with you the story of how one heroic person discovered his own authenticity and went on to become one of the most important public speakers in American history and a close confidant of President Lincoln.

Frederick Douglass was a self-educated and enlightened slave in North Carolina and Maryland who suffered severely at the hands of violent and cruel slave owners. Charting a daring course to freedom, he landed in Massachusetts, where he began working as a freeman caulker in a prosperous northern shipbuilding seaport. Sensing he had more to offer than his journeyman skills and feeling a strong desire to speak out publicly for the abolition of slavery, Douglass felt moved and was encouraged by others to begin his career in oratory. This is the inspiring way he describes the discovery of his authentic self and his own voice and how he began his speaking career. He literally shed the slave identity for his natural-born one, and that gave him true liberation to pursue his calling. Here he explains his transformation in his own words.

> *While attending an anti-slavery convention at Nantucket...I felt strongly moved to speak...It was a severe cross and I took it up reluctantly. The truth was, I felt myself a slave, and the idea of speaking to white people weighed me down. I spoke but a few moments, when I felt a degree of freedom, and said what I desired with considerable ease. From that time until now, I have been engaged in pleading the cause of my brethren—with what success, and with what devotion, I leave those acquainted with my labors to decide.* (From *Narrative of the Life of Frederick Douglass, An American Slave.*)

Helpful Steps to Gaining Personal Confidence

William Shakespeare may have been our noblest guide and inspiration on this topic when he wrote, for his character Polonius in his play *Hamlet*: "This above all: to thine own self be true, and it must follow, as the night the day, thou canst not then be false to any man. Farewell, my blessing season this in thee!"

Frederick Douglass was known as a masterful speaker who influenced the
end of slavery.

Shakespeare surely had many inauthentic characters in his plays and recognized and created authentic speakers as well. He knew the difference, and this made his plays multidimensional. In this we can also see why acting and oration are two sides of the same coin—though this is lost on a majority of speakers. In reality all public speaking is performance.

In acting, if the performer does not interpret the character accurately, there is little believability. The same can be said of the public speaker. Every speech, no matter how small and insignificant, should always be approached as a performance or a gift from the speaker to the audience. Shakespeare confirms this too, in his speech penned for Jaques in another of his plays, *As You Like It*, when he says,

"All the world's a stage, And all the men and women merely players; They have their exits and their entrances, And one man in his time plays many parts."

Becoming authentic is a personal, private, and inner accomplishment expressed in an outward, social, or public way. Achieving a degree of self-knowledge is a major accomplishment and involves a lifelong learning process that provides something like a ladder that helps you climb the rungs represented by the seven objectives below.

These seven elements, goals, or steps that may help us define ourselves as authentic in our role as a public speaker are articulated below. To achieve even some of these traits will show you are rising on the authenticity scale and that you are making better speeches because of this exercise. No one achieves a perfect score on all points, just as very few people become exceptional speakers overnight. Like life itself, it takes practice!

1. Define your identity, not as a Wiki page of statistics meant for the public, but define your character for yourself. Write it down in a notebook, laptop, phone, or piece of paper where you can look at it and think about it. You might even revise it, because we are, each of us, a developing story, a work in progress. Paint a self-portrait in words and have a good look at it. If you can't figure yourself out, then how would you expect anyone else to understand you? The best speakers have a grasp on this, and their words emanate from who they are and represent their character. It gives them a confidence that is attractive to the audience—especially anyone looking for answers and leadership.

2. Make every effort to be honest in your discovery of personal facts and dispassionate about finding the truth, not in just repeating the opinions of others—and express these in candid terms in your talk. Live a life as close to the ideals you are asking other people to live by—as may be expressed in the content of your speech.

3. Live some type of what I call an "interpretive" life. That means you are thinking about your life as you live it, including interpreting for yourself what you discover, see, and experience, as it relates to the lives of others and as

you reflect on and think about these issues with depth and objectivity. Dive beneath the surface issues of living.

4. Strive to be personally secure enough to reveal some vulnerability and uncertainty in your thinking and life that allows some space and availability for the outside, the audience, to come into your life to help you figure things out.

5. Let your audience know you need and value them, and that you are a fellow traveler, never above or more privileged than anyone listening to you. There is nothing that digs a wider and deeper trench between a speaker and the audience than to express personal superiority or disdain for your listeners.

6. Do not preach or tell others how to live their lives. Share your story of struggle and accomplishment in a way that people can respect you and emulate your journey for themselves, but never for personal aggrandizement. Put down your personal need to control others through your speech. Educate and inspire by example.

7. To be authentic never means to be weak or unconfident. Rather, your confidence lies in the fact that you know yourself, or at least are striving to, and that you are aware of this process and are grateful for it and that you know what you believe. Being authentic is not so much about being proud as it is being humble. Humility is an attractive and attracting quality.

Outward Expressions of Inner Authenticity

In addition to developing your authentic inner self, you also deliver it, in part, through your body language. The goal is to have the two synchronized. The greater the degree of self-knowledge, the more comfortable you will be in your own skin, and the more confidence and ease you will convey. Your audience is watching you, and they will take their cue about nervousness or discomfort from you. If you lose your place, sneeze, move your body unnecessarily, or suddenly grab the podium, it can send alarm bells and distract the audience, even though these may seem natural to you. Always be conscious of the audience and their comfort, while at the same time you are focused on your message.

Being a speaker is a multitasking job. Don't be surprised that as you speak and are absorbed in the words and concepts of your speech, your conscious thought will be hard at work on many levels. You will think about where your phone is, with whom you are having dinner, whether or not you paid a bill on time, or if your friend, who said she would attend, is in the audience or not. Try as you like to ward off these intrusive distractions, they are guaranteed to present themselves, because your mind is a multitasking operation—a computer with several apps open synchronously. Awareness of this is just the right antidote to its probable distraction.

When it raises its voice, and it will, your thought should mentally say back to it, "I know you are going right on with your random thoughts and messages, but I am staying focused on the important information I am sharing with the audience.

You can go on talking to me, but I will not be listening to you or be distracted." You may be surprised but you can actually talk to your intruding sub-consciousness at the same time you are delivering an important message on a conscious level. After you address that voice, then it's a good idea to increase your energy level and force of delivery just as if you were in a competitive drag race, and you leave your annoying and distracting competing thought in the dust as you accelerate away from it.

This scenario has happened to me hundreds of times, right while I am on the dais. And I know that President Reagan experienced this as well. I can imagine, with his somewhat halting manner of speaking, that President Trump has multiple competing ideas roaming around in his brain, like popcorn, while he is speaking. I would say that he is probably prone to distraction while speaking and has had to enforce a discipline like never before as president. Being confined to a teleprompter is good for his discipline as an orator, but it may not be easy for him. Reagan and the teleprompter had a long and favorable association. Making it work for any speaker is a complex process that Reagan had long mastered.

Body Language

The goal for your body language is to put the audience at ease. This means you must at least appear to be at ease yourself. Body language is how the audience reads or interprets your physical movements in relation to your message delivery. It's how your body represents on the outside what you are thinking on the inside and how your movements represent your self-image. Your target is to help the audience become receptive to your message and content without your body interfering with this process or transmission. In principle, you have spent a significant amount of time on research and on crafting the script, so you want to achieve maximum potential attention and absorption.

First, as you approach the stage or area where you will present, you should do so with energy and enthusiasm. You should feel a sense of delight or at least positive anticipation and gratitude for this opportunity to present—even if you are reporting poor earnings, a security breach, or something other than good news. If you are able, and there are stairs up to the platform, tread carefully but with energy. Grab the handrail, if available, even if you think it is not needed. Tripping on the steps does not send the right message for your opening. If you are seated on stage while you are introduced, look directly at your host and smile with appreciation for the introduction. Sit up straight. Do not cross your legs at the knees. Sit comfortably with the ankles crossed and legs together.

A good rule of thumb, which is often not observed, is to always look at the person on stage who has the speaking role at any time. This should be easy, but you often find the principal speaker's eyes darting everywhere while being introduced. The truth is that the audience is looking at you to know how to behave. This shows the audience where to look as well. Stand still. Moving your body anxiously or unnecessarily will take energy away from you and may result in the audience feeling that you have lost power, which could lessen their desire to listen to you. My advice to my students is to remain in a stationary position when speaking. Moving across the stage, which is somewhat popular today, can take away from the focus of the audience on you and take some power away from your presentation.

I have only known one speaker, Daniel Pink, who could command the full stage, moving around actively while speaking with a remote lavalier microphone; and because of his magnetic message and fascinating way of talking, he commands you follow him. He adds energy and urgency to his talks. You don't want to miss one word of what he says. I have had an opportunity to become acquainted with Dan. He has become one of the top influencers on management and education in the world. He tells you his life story and then pulls you in with new thoughts and new thinking in rapid-fire succession and then makes these new ideas logical and stimulating. He applies them to your own situation and you believe in him and trust him. He is not taking anything from you, he is constantly giving to you. His body movements undergird and support the energy of his ideas. Watch him on YouTube, and I am sure you will agree.

When it comes time for you to speak, take immediate command as if you have something of urgent value to communicate. Stand with your shoulders back and your neck pushed back against your collar or dress. Make sure your hair is not in your eyes or falling in your face. Try not to touch your hair or face while you are speaking. You want to project an air of confidence and ease so your audience will be at ease and confident in you. For women especially, every time you touch your hair you lose power with the audience.

If you suffer from a disability or discomfort that would make standing at a podium uncomfortable or dangerous, rather than struggle with it, share with the audience that you are going to speak to them seated. Better to explain yourself than to leave your audience guessing or concerned about you or your health. That could become the big news story of the event rather than your message. Drawing your audience up close in a personal way like this may make them listen more intently.

Don't be afraid to smile. Your subject may be serious and not lighthearted, but a genuine smile doesn't hurt except in the most somber and grave situations. Smiling changes and brightens your voice quality and tone. Smiling also pushes your cheekbones up to make you look younger and generally pushes modest blood flow to the surface to give you some color. Smiling with your eyes is also a good trick. Try it. It works. Smiles or modest animation bring out the cameras, which is good and connects you to the audience. You want them to know you don't feel tortured by being in the presenter's seat—even though you might be.

Eye Contact

The politicians' trick today, especially when there are cameras rolling, is to pretend or imply that they are seeing familiar faces in the audience as they recognize and point to them. It makes for excellent camera footage and photo ops because it makes the politician smile and adds animation to what could be a dour and boring pictorial record. Hillary Clinton is a master at this. When you observe her at almost any event you will know what I mean. I became a keen observer of this tactic and recorded other politicians copying this strategy. It makes good theater and builds that all-important bridge with the audience.

Even more, if you happen to be present at the event, or even observing at a distance, it elevates your opinion of yourself when the political leader appears to acknowledge a personal relationship with people there who might also be rubbing shoulders with you. It also plays a trick on you to make you think that the candidate or politician is well liked by many people at the event and very popular to have all those friends. The outside observer can be taken in by this strategy. For the everyday speaker, like you and me, gestures like that would be unthinkable and perceived as egocentric and off-putting for a nonpolitical speaker or even a politician not running for the highest office in the land. Waving should be reserved for officeholders or candidates for the head of state job.

A rule for eye contact, especially in a smaller venue, is to focus on sections of the crowd intently and earnestly but never to remain in eye contact too long with any individual. That would be seen as choosing favorites and cutting others in the audience out. It also may unnerve the individual on whom you focus. A good rule is to look at individuals slightly above eye level or at their foreheads and to also look on sections of the auditorium where not every seat may be filled, to give the impression that you have a standing-room-only crowd. In the theater, actors are trained to look at the tops of the heads of people in the audience.

Often when I am speaking in a hall with a balcony, although there may be no one seated there, I am looking up, letting my eyes roam around the room embracing everyone in my mental and physical eyesight. Eye contact is an expression of interest in the audience and an authentic genialness coming from your heart to theirs. In some ancient literature, eyes and heart were linked in meaning. If you notice someone special to you in the audience or known to you in some way, it is perfectly fine to give them a small smile when you are talking and come across their face.

Again, with eye contact you are building that bridge and bringing down a wall of division. When you conclude your speech and step down from the podium, you would naturally resume strong and intent eye contact with any individual with whom you are speaking. There is nothing more unnerving and disconcerting than to have the person you are speaking with one-on-one dart their eyes in every direction but your face.

Your Physical Appearance

Never forget, as a speaker, people are watching you, assessing you, sizing you up, and, yes, judging you. You are on display when you are making a speech. I do not say that to scare you more than you are already, but to toughen you, to prepare you for scrutiny. You may not think of yourself as a celebrity, but for the moments you are on stage, or behind the lens of a video camera or phone, you are—even if you are standing in an elementary school gym and delivering a few brief comments to parents. There will be many in your audience who will judge what you are wearing, your haircut or hairstyle and color, your makeup, facial hair, whether or not you appear well put together or casual about what you wear. Whether you are overweight or trim, buff or of average build. It goes with the job.

You are not necessarily dressing to impress your audience, but you are dressing to express your respect for them. They may have traveled a long distance to hear you or made a significant effort to be in the hall. They may have made an effort with their attire to be presentable. You are dressing to make your audience feel important, alert, worthy of your message and your presence. You dress thoughtfully because what you have to say is thoughtful and important to you and valuable to the audience.

When you are on stage, you are typically in a brighter, sometimes harsher, light. If you appear on television or in video, that is when you are typically made up by a makeup artist. The camera is unforgiving of any blemishes or skin irregularities or a dark beard. Note to men: do not attempt to escape the makeup application under any circumstance. Makeup artists are skilled at what they do, and they want you to make your best appearance and are highly trained and skilled at it—making it happen in just the right way. On camera you will look natural after you have the required makeup applied. You will seem inexperienced or immature if you resist it, and you surely won't look as good without it.

One time I appeared on several network early morning shows in rapid succession all on one day and was made up at 4:40 a.m. I was hungry about eleven a.m., so I walked across the street to a cafe in Rockefeller Center. While I was eating I suddenly realized that I was fully made up and had not taken off the stage makeup. My first reaction was alarm and embarrassment until I realized no one even noticed it, and if they did, they didn't care—especially in a city with as much diversity and as many colorful people as New York.

One last piece of personal advice for how your face appears. For both men and women, you should install in your own bathroom, and regularly consult, a magnifying mirror. For men this helps with areas you may not have completely shaved or trimmed, including unwanted hair or overgrown eyebrows. If you cannot stand to look at yourself close up, you are not yet ready for prime time. A magnifying mirror is essential. Always travel with one in your suitcase. For women, from a distance your color will wash out in front of an audience, so you will want to apply more color than usual. You want to look alive and energetic. I have had students who resist my advice on this and look bland on stage and sometimes sallow. It is distracting. Think of your audience and the photos you will inevitably want to post. Prepare yourself!

Before you depart for your engagement, at home or in your hotel, look at yourself in the mirror in a brightly lit room and realize that under the lights, you may fade out if you wear light colors. Fair-haired and fair-skinned people should wear strong, darker colors. No one should wear patterned clothing, especially if the speech will be recorded or broadcast. Bold stripes are out. Darker colors on anyone will make them appear more serious and important and may be taken that way by the audience. Darker colors will make you appear slimmer, if you want that effect. Similarly, do not wear clothing that is too tight or too small for your frame, even though many of the female newsreaders and talk show hosts on FOX network do this all the time. It may be a part of the FOX winning formula, but it still makes some people uncomfortable.

Wear durable deodorant. Performing onstage will absolutely effect a rise in your body temperature and you will perspire. After all, you are hard at work. This is not something you want to reveal to your audience. Women might want to wear dress shields and men to wear undershirts. Do not wear jewelry that dangles, makes noise, interferes with amplification, or sparkles to distraction. It is wise to remove your watch as it could catch on the edge of the podium. Leave it home or in your pocket or place it on the podium where you can observe the passing time but not be distracted by it.

Do not wear clothing that would separate you from your audience, nothing too audacious. You want your audience to relate to you. If your objective is to appear unconventional in your attire, then you might get credit for creativity, but you may also bring down the fourth wall of division from some in the audience who might criticize you. If you have ever watched celebrities parading on the red carpet for the annual Metropolitan Museum Costume Exhibit Gala in New York, while these may be extraordinary people of accomplishment in their fields, they may not be people you would necessarily invite to deliver, nor would you listen to them giving, a serious speech on US-China trade policy or the rise and fall of the dollar versus the euro. They are displaying colorful clothing for our entertainment and delight as well as paid advertising and influencing.

If you are speaking in a foreign country, you may need to consult with an in-country expert on protocol and cultural norms. You do not want what you wear to offend your hosts. Even though you may not be a president of a country, you may be president of a company or organization, and your clothing mistakes could harm your negotiation or how you are received. In some countries specific colors have special meaning. While most unyielding protocol rules have liberalized in the global economy, there are still customs to adhere to and respect. Red, with some exceptions, is universally considered a color of power and happiness. Red is a color people associate with. Blue brings the temperature down.

For women, if you are televised or taped, a white or cream dress or blouse will reflect more light onto your face, which is flattering and erases wrinkles. I observed the dramatic impact of light while managing a *Vogue* magazine cover photo shoot upstairs in the White House family quarters by the famed British photographer Norman Parkinson. He illustrated and taught me the power of light by applying almost no makeup to his subject (male or female)—who in this shoot was the first lady—by flooding her face with light shining upward from the floor onto her face. The result was a dramatic example of the power of light to make subjects appear more youthful and alive. My daughter, Claire Harvey, who is a professional photographer, knows this and uses this strategy to flatter her subjects. Light has a natural effect but must be deployed skillfully and knowingly.

So, remember as a speaker, if possible, to ask for the podium to be well lighted. This approach might seem counterintuitive to you, thinking that you would rather be seen in a poorly lit situation, to hide flaws, but the reverse is true. For the focus and value of your topic, make sure the stage, and the podium specifically, are well lighted if you possibly can. The better the light, the more easily our audience will be able to focus on you, and they will be more alert to your content and as a side effect, the better you will look, in person and in photographs.

In *summary*, here are the best ten rules for clothing on the podium.

1. Select your clothing to relate to the audience, not to alarm or separate you or to detract from your message.

2. Wear darker clothing to appear more serious, trim, powerful.

3. For women, wear white or cream near the face to reflect light. Barbara Bush used a pearl necklace to pull this off and was rarely seen without it.

4. Make sure your clothing fits: not too tight or loose. For women, not too short or revealing. All these things take the focus off your message and place it on you—which is not optimal.

5. If you wear a tie, make absolutely certain it is pulled up tight to the neck and does not sag down on your shirt to make you look sloppy. For tie color, generally wear a plain, strong, complementary color. Your shirt collar should be high on your neck to present a more youthful and energetic appearance. If you wear a pocket square in your suit jacket, make it discreet and not floppy or flamboyant. These are distractions.

6. Always wear your best attire, clothing that you like and that makes you feel good about yourself. If you are in doubt or fussing about your selection, this indecisiveness could carry over into your delivery. You need your clothes to be a confidence builder. So make a good decision about your outfit, and then feel confident about it.

7. Do not wear stripes, flowered patterns, dark shirts with suits, dangling jewelry, big rings (unless it's a Super Bowl one), or even watches.

8. If you are a regular speaker, develop a few "uniforms" that work for you and wear them again and again. They become supportive friends, and will generally only be seen by one audience at a time. If you travel for speaking, always hang your outfits on hangers and wrap them in plastic dry cleaner bags to keep them wrinkle free in your suitcase. Bring enough outfits to make up for a coffee spill or tear in your clothing. You may not have time while on the road to take something to the cleaners or to have a repair completed or even to purchase something new.

9. Always plan ahead for your wardrobe—even men. If you are on an important speaking tour, take a journal and record what you wore on each occasion or simply take a picture of your outfit on your phone. For many men this is not an issue, but it may be the reverse for women, who may need to coordinate their outfits with others on the podium, including the introducer. The rule is to be thoughtful of others, and if you have the opportunity to plan ahead, avoid clashing on the podium.

10. Clothing should represent the authentic you, and being authentic includes your consideration of your listening audience. Radical outfits may be selected or preferred by some speakers because they want to make a point, even artistically, but ask yourself what you want to achieve in the long run—to be remembered for what you wore or what you said. Of course, dressing elegantly can lift the entire occasion. Dressing in causal clothing to match what many people wear on airplanes today will lower the expectations for your message and delivery—unless you are a physical trainer or sports figure.

Posture

Being a speaker provides you the opportunity to improve the way you stand and move, including the way you place your arms and legs. Too many hours over a laptop or screen result in rounded shoulders that make a person appear weak or stooped. Posture is another way to convey self-confidence and knowledge and to deliver authenticity. To stand straight may require some stretching and exercise to maintain strength. It also requires correctly fitting clothes and especially shoes. For the speaker, shoes are important, so make them comfortable and supportive of good posture.

Recently I coached a gentleman who looked like Richard Gere. That was the good part. The bad part was that he had developed the habit of sinking his chin into his chest when speaking, while his hair was falling down covering almost all of his forehead. It was difficult for the audience to hear him because his voice was trending downward toward the floor because of the position of his chin and mouth. I pushed his chin up, his neck back against his shirt collar, and had him gel his hair back somewhat. He was a new man! Standing taller with his face open and facing into the audience he could be seen and heard clearly for the first time. The lights lit up his face, where before they had a hard time finding it. He was now not hiding but front-facing. It completely changed the way the audience saw and heard him. It was a striking but simple transformation, and of course it completely changed his presentation and its effectiveness.

You can try this yourself by standing in front of a mirror. Before you make any physical assessment and change, ask yourself: is what I have to say important to the audience? If you answer in the affirmative, then transform your body to fit the task. Stand back against a wall and make sure your shoulder blades touch the wall, with your heels against the baseboard. Place the palms of your hands against the wall as well. Now lift your chin. Now walk forward into the mirror and start speaking. See and hear the change in how you convey and deliver your remarks. If you practice this enough, it will become your standard way of walking and talking, and it will add energy and tone to your presentation.

When you are at the podium, do not lock your legs at the knees under any circumstances. It could stop blood flow and cause fainting. Keep your toes and legs moving lightly in an inconspicuous but consistent way while you speak. If you are speaking without a podium and nowhere to hide, you can still keep your toes moving. This is a good reason not to wear sandals or open-toed shoes.

A serious way to improve posture and breathing is through

regular exercise like yoga or Pilates. Any type of aerobic exercise will help with breathing and breath control as well—even walking. Stretching or being stretched in massage regularly will also help. Travel, which is often paired with speaking tours, is not the friend of great posture. If you want to have an elevating presentation, make sure you attempt to elevate your posture. It will affect the tone of your voice as well as your appearance. Of course, stay hydrated but not over-hydrated.

Hand Gestures

When standing behind a desk or podium, rest your hands easily on it or at your side. If you do not have a podium in front of you, hand gestures may be awkward and a challenge to regulate. Here is the rule: hand gestures are used as punctuation. For most of your speech, keep your hands at your side or rest them on a tabletop or lectern. When you reach points in your speech where there is punctuation that stresses interesting issues or numbered points, use your hands to enforce a point or paint a picture.

For example, let's say you are speaking of four points. You might hold up four fingers to stress that number. If you are speaking of a beautiful and sweeping horizon, you might sweep your hand in front of you and the audience to illustrate the sweep of what you saw. If you ask a question, you might raise your arms halfway up your body as if you are bracketing the question. If you want to embrace the audience and are speaking of everyone coming together for a purpose, you might raise and widen your arms as if you were going to give the whole audience a collective hug.

Discipline yourself not to make excessive hand gestures. It may take effort over time to accomplish this. Watch yourself in a mirror practicing your speech. If you have a tendency toward using your hands too much, you might be convinced to break the habit. Too much hand gesturing will weaken the seriousness of what you are saying and distract the audience. For men especially, rather than standing awkwardly and not knowing what to do with their hands, they might clasp them behind their back, put one hand in a pants pocket, or simply clasp them in front. The best rule is to err on the side of fewer hand gestures.

Can Your Voice Fill the Hall?

Some individuals who have a small voice fear they can never be great speakers. That is untrue. It is possible to change the tone and size of your voice. But it takes effort. Recently I worked with a gentleman whom we will call Ned who had a high-pitched voice that sounded unnatural. Few of us like the sound of our own voice when we hear it recorded and played back to us. Ned was no exception to this rule. I explained to him that deeper voices with a lower octave pitch are more easily heard by the human ear and are better transmitted by amplification. To lower his voice, one that he had been using for decades, we had to attempt to orient a new breath pattern up from his stomach to open his vocal pathways and, through practice, to stop him from inhaling exclusively through his nose. As an exercise I asked him to hold a basketball and press it firmly against his stomach facing a wall. Next I had him lean into the ball to put pressure on his belly, forcing warm air up from the gut, and then to breathe deeply. Then I asked him to try to sing some low notes, which I gave him. He was amazed that he could actually speak at the lower pitch.

Then I asked him to play recorded speeches by low-pitched speakers and to listen to music sung by baritones and basses. These are essential tools because, of course, the voice is linked to the ear. I wanted Ned to hear low tones so he could copy them. Your voice is a copier. In fact, I suffer from *involuntary* musical ear. This means that, especially when traveling to a region that has a distinct language inflection, I may unintentionally speak using that unique colloquial manner. It has been an embarrassment to my family when, ordering in a restaurant in the Deep South for example, I randomly blurt out something that mimics the waiter's way of speaking. They think I am making fun of the person I am copying, but I have tried to convince them I am not.

For Ned, I asked him to *voluntarily* copy voices, as a good way to accelerate the change. Now he has daily exercises to perform, and if he keeps at it and practices speaking from the stomach and listening to, copying, and applying the lower octaves, he can be a winner and ultimately be better heard, even in a large room. Ned stands a chance of owning the room.

Some people, like Trump, are masters at being heard. For example, his voice fills up a big space. Everyone hears precisely what he is saying because he wants them to—even though the timbre is not in the lower ranges. If he thinks you might have missed something, he repeats himself. He pushes a lot of air through his lungs and adds a staccato to many of his words and also strings—them—out. I would call this barking it out—but it works. What he says gets into the ears, hearts, and minds of his listeners.

Reagan spoke in a lower-pitched voice with less drama, and that drew the listener to him. His was not an excited tone but more of a grave one, when called for. Both voices are easily identified as belonging to these two unique individuals, and are a part of their trademarks. Both voices have been useful to and provided plenty of valuable work to comedians and others who portray the iconic inflections and cadences of both men. Most of us have identifiable voices as an imprint of our identity. Most of us have authentic ways of speaking that originated in patterns copied from our parents, the region of the country or world where we were born and first learned to speak, and from those around us when we were first articulating sound. As babies we mimic the sounds of others, and from these first few words we develop a speaking vocabulary.

Some of us give speeches in languages other than our native tongue. This presents special challenges for the audience, and as a result the speaker may want to slow the oration down. It might even be a good idea to explain to your audience that English is not your native language so with fair warning the audience will be prepared and more forgiving. If your English is not at an easily discernible level, it may be a good idea to have a native English speaker read your talk. The audience may appreciate hearing it clearly and also appreciate you more for being the author. What I have said about native English speakers applies, of course, to any native language speaker presenting to an audience whose first language the speaker does not share. Personally, I have a strong preference for speakers who speak with accented English. It makes me listen more closely, and it makes the presentation more interesting.

Almost all presentation spaces have electronic amplification available. Please do not start your talk by asking if the audience can hear you. It dilutes your powerful start. You should be able to discern if you can be heard by simply listening to the volume of your voice in the hall. Make certain you speak directly into the tip of the mic. If the amplification does not make your voice heard (even though you will have tested it beforehand), speak louder and pretend you are saving the life of someone in the back row. If that does not correct the problem, then ask that it be corrected electronically and stop your speech until it is.

In all cases where it is possible, require a sound and lighting technician to be on hand at the start and during your presentation. This is an added cost for the host organization, but the quality of your remarks may depend upon it, and the enjoyment of the audience will follow, making a greater success for the organization. I have spoken at conferences and meetings where professional services for lighting and amplification varied. To the extent possible, take control of this situation yourself and don't worry about the possibility of stepping on the toes of your host organization. If you are speaking from a podium, you might also ask for a light to be turned on at the podium or stage lighting focused on it. Making a delivery in the dark is not an option. Many hosts simply are not educated in or aware of staging protocol but you should be. Your host and your audience will appreciate your asking for more lighting or better sound even though you may be reticent to step in. Experienced speakers make their requirements for sound and lighting in advance.

Rapid and Accelerated Delivery

You may have noticed that among newsreaders on network shows, some read faster than others. David Muir introduced accelerated delivery to evening news when he began his tenure at ABC. It may have helped his appeal to a younger generation, which prizes fast talking. Muir can typically report on more stories in the airtime allotted him, and he moves the telecast along faster. The reason this works is because the human mind can process faster than the lips/mouth can speak. This is why there can be criticism of slow or boring speakers putting people in the audience to sleep. Fast talkers like David Muir do not have that problem.

There is another unique benefit to rapid delivery. It makes you seem smarter to the audience, and it makes them remain focused on what you are saying and race to keep pace with you. Fast talking aligned with dramatic and appropriate pauses may be the best approach to keeping your audience right with you in your delivery. This is what I call "sprinter delivery"— as if you are running a race in short bursts of energy, allowing yourself and the audience intermediate moments to stop and rest the mind and assess what has been delivered. Talking fast also reminds the audience that you have an urgent message, a timely one needing their attention, and you have worked hard to master your topic or subject. Finding a useful and productive rhythm is what you most need. There are times that require a slower, more dramatic pace, but combining these tempos is what works best.

CHAPTER FOUR

Defeating Fear

Fear is pain arising from the anticipation of evil.

—Aristotle

Courage is knowing what not to fear.

—Plato

The mind is a wonderful thing. It starts the minute you are born and never stops until you get up to speak in public!

—Roscoe Drummond

What Is Fear and Where Does It Come From?

If you learn only one thing from this book, it should be how to master fear. Once you master fear, you have tamed the most formidable foe of your becoming an eloquent and creditable public speaker. It may take several rounds to wholly defeat this muscle-bound and scary tyrant, because fear is like a persistent and unrelenting boxing opponent—who is usually rising during the count and is right back at you with an annoying right jab to your self-confidence once again. Fear is an unreasonable opponent, making demands, calling the shots, basically controlling your ability to be a master of many things.

Fear can sideline you occasionally or keep you out of competition completely. It may arise suddenly, mysteriously, and apparently without cause. It is irrational and resists exposure because it flourishes in darkness. It has existed from all creation and has been spoken and written about, illustrated in great art as well as cartoons, analyzed, fought, destroyed and risen again, triumphed, and been the cause of many hours of psychiatric visits and counseling. Even our originators of rhetoric, Aristotle and Plato, have spoken about it and succumbed to it on occasion. Just as they introduced the laws of oratory in Greece, they saw how fear struck down their own students. Aristotle, the great teacher of rhetoric, sustained a lifelong fear of speaking himself because of a debilitating stammer.

In its constructive uses as an intuition, fear can sense imminent danger and can save a life. To listen to fear and adhere to its warnings can be lifesaving. On the other hand, when fear is engineered by irrationality, it is destructive. These are two different mind-forces. It is wise to carefully avoid the open flame for fear of being burned on the stove. But it is irrational to avoid using the stove for cooking just because you are controlled by the fear of thinking you might hurt yourself. Fear is not just being afraid of something. It is a force that attempts to draw you inward, to restrict you, to tighten the muscles and limit the bloodflow.

Most importantly, fear is a separator. Fear is the lever that can divide you from your audience right when you should feel united with your audience waiting to hear from you. Any wall of fear makes you self-conscious and makes you fear what the audience might think of you. This is how it begins its campaign to silence you and your message. This is how it attempts to rule over you. Unless you defeat it, fear may continue its drumbeat until it finally defeats you and relegates you to silence. Never forget that fear is not caused by your audience, so look straight at them and face down that idea. The fear is in your own or the speaker's mind. Your audience is nothing to fear at all.

Reagan provides an excellent example of someone who confronted fear and refused to be controlled by it. He did not fear public speaking, not just because he had performed in front of a camera hundreds of times, as some people might suggest, but because he truly did not care what people in the audience thought of him. He surely wanted to do his best, to inspire, and to make an effective speech, but he was not obsessed with how the audience felt about him or what he said. He was not available or susceptible to the audience in this way, and so he was not fearful of speaking or how an audience might harm him or his reputation.

When I learned this about him, it seemed to me an almost impossible achievement, and a new type of leadership. Most people I interacted with would surely admit to having some sensitivity to what the audience thought of their manner of speaking and their content. Thinking more about this, it occurred to me that if a leader like Reagan did not care what people in the audience thought of him, then he would not be unduly influenced by them to take one or another position on public policy or to compromise.

That began to solidify in my mind as the highest type of leadership. That is not to say that great leaders do not need flexibility and the ability to listen to the developing and evolving or changing needs of the people they lead. I had seen how immoveable Reagan was when it came to his principles and ideals. Now I had more insight into why and how this immunity to what people thought of him and a lack of need to please an audience had developed in him.

Out of all the lessons in this book, if you learn to master fear you will be on the road to eloquence. Here is an even more important and transforming promise and goal: studying, working, practicing to become articulate by knowing yourself and your genuine identity will provide you with a fearless life that will affect and improve every single aspect of your life— not just public speaking skills alone. Time and time again as I've coached students, they have told me that this work has transformed their lives. Why? Because learning to speak confidently requires changes in aspects of your life that have inhibited you in other ways as well.

Identifying insecurities, shifting from a focus on self to a focus on others (audiences) and being freed from fear can set you on a growth trajectory—leaving a lot of undesirable traits and stress behind. Learning to speak is a gift that delivers on all cylinders. This is also why learning to become a public speaker is the best medicine for many ills and provides you with the artillery to confront and destroy limitations. Your commitment to the lessons of oratory and their mastery will help you rid yourself of inhibitors in many departments of life.

Fear Is More Than Being Afraid

When we were little we were afraid of the dark, of ghosts, of the wicked witch, of learning to ride a bicycle or being left home with a babysitter. These fears were overcome mostly by growing out of them, living half our life in the dark at night, learning that ghosts are imaginary, and so on. Being afraid can be something you educate yourself out of. When I first joined the swim team in seventh grade, I was afraid of the high dive but, through repetitive diving practice, learned to overcome being afraid. When I first skied on black diamond runs, I was afraid but learned through forging ahead that I could ski mostly unafraid. Today I look at skydivers and think I could never do that, even as I watched President George H. W. Bush dive from an airplane, the last time at age ninety, and apparently without fear. When I watch rock climbers scale vertical formations without safety belts and ropes, it is hard to imagine accomplishing a feat like that. But I also understand that fear would bring them down. They cannot allow themselves the luxury of being fearful.

The same could be said of the extraordinary courage displayed by the men and women of the military who head into combat afraid of what might lurk around any corner or what might explode in the very ground they traverse in war zones. Navy Seals have learned how to grapple with and overcome being afraid using a number of strategies including breathing, meditation, laughter, or just talking back to the fear. As former commander James Waters says, "We spend seventy-five percent of our time preparing and practicing, and twenty-five percent on the deployment so by the time they are facing real danger they are used to what might happen and can be in command of the situation without being intimidated by it or being afraid." They know that fear is the enemy.

I have become acquainted with one of the top Ironman

competitors in the world and I stand in awe of the mountains he has conquered by not letting fear stand in the way of Herculean accomplishment. He also rowed a wooden boat with no auxiliary power from California to Hawaii, breaking a world record. Extreme sports enthusiasts seek the thrill of overcoming being afraid and are always looking for new barriers to break down.

Here is how Danny Harf, well-known extreme sports promoter, describes his love of extreme sports:

I love that pursuit of progression. Trying to overcome something that scared me and accomplishing what I had set out to do. Succeed or fail, it's about getting outside of your comfort zone. The only way to go forward is to be willing to take that next step.

Fear of public speaking seems to pale in complexity and seriousness next to some of these awesome accomplishments. And yet personal fear is something more complex and devilish than just being afraid. Being afraid is typically about something outside of yourself and your identity. Being afraid can be educated around or dealt with through experience. Fear, however, strikes at the more profoundly personally threatening areas of how we view ourselves in relation to a task or other people. Some of these issues are perceived as unfixable challenges to the complex soul of a person.

Sounds scary and unsolvable, right? We will see how it can be brought down and what the formula is to get us to the finish line of final freedom from fear that will help unleash confident speaking.

What Are the Effects of Fear and Who Exhibits Them?

Here are a few of the effects and signs of fear that might be observable as it relates to public speaking:

- Reticence to speak up in public and avoiding all opportunities to present
- Shyness and excessive concern about content
- Extreme sensitivity and perfectionism
- Self-centeredness and self-condemnation
- Halting and imprecise speech patterns
- Stammering, dizziness
- Unconfident, low-volume speaking voice
- Avoiding opportunities to present or ask questions in a group setting
- Avoidance of opportunities to share and speak up
- Nervousness and irregular breathing
- Sweating, perspiration, coughing, or clearing of the throat unnecessarily
- Need to drink water during a speech
- Extreme fear of being criticized
- Losing your place in thought or stream of consciousness
- Excessive fretting over personal appearance, clothing, or voice quality.

If you exhibit these tendencies, you are not alone. As we have seen, these are people from all walks of life. Most people like to keep these insecurities private, hoping they will never be asked to speak. Fear can target anyone indiscriminately, and yet most people can live their lives without ever being forced to deal with it in relation to public speaking because they are not called upon for these skills.

If you have ever watched an Academy Awards show, you may observe an award-winning actor who, having assumed on-screen roles for which she portrays a character masterfully, might lack the ability to speak off the cuff and unscripted when receiving their award. Most of these actors whom we associate with coolness and competence will readily admit to nervousness to the point of embarrassment and confusion when called on stage to make an acceptance speech. Here are just a few of the surprising bold-face names you might know of from the fields of business, politics, and film and throughout history who openly admit to having been fearful of public speaking.

These are people who have talked about working to master their fear and succeeded.

Moses	Jimmy Stewart
Bruce Willis	Joel Osteen
Eleanor Roosevelt	Sir Isaac Newton
Julia Roberts	Mahatma Gandhi
Sigmund Freud	Mark Zuckerberg
Harrison Ford	Thomas Jefferson
Princess Diana	Samuel L. Jackson
Tiger Woods	Abraham Lincoln
Warren Buffett	Nicole Kidman

Practical Steps to Master Fear

Let's begin by starting a personal and private journal with four chapters and a foreword, and let's call it:

MY FEAR OF PUBLIC SPEAKING
MASTERY BOOK

Journal Foreword

On the first page of your journal, I want you to write this line boldly. It's really a promise to yourself:

**I AM ON MY WAY TO BECOMING A
BRILLIANT, SOUGHT-AFTER PUBLIC
SPEAKER. NOTHING WILL KEEP ME FROM
REACHING THIS GOAL.**

Journal Chapter One: The Simple List of Fears

Journaling is a great place to begin. Plunge right in. In the early days of your journaling a flood of ideas will come to you. In the middle days it may be tougher, and as you near the end of the course you will also have a new flood of ideas you want to cram in—including things you may have forgotten to address. Your journal is a private and nonthreatening world, and you can trust your journal to keep your confidences.

In journaling you are thinking and talking to yourself—how great is that! It's a start at becoming better acquainted with you. Introducing yourself to you. Starting on the course of self-knowledge. Most people have never even taken the time to be self-reflective in a calm way. Most self-examination comes in a restive or stressful situation when there may be a personal crisis of some kind, like divorce—when people might begin to examine their attitudes and behavior. We are largely ignorant of who we are. The day you start journaling with this purpose in mind is the day you begin to become better acquainted with the person you are or have become. It may not all be pretty to look at; some of it may even be shocking or ugly. You may not like what you write, but it's the first step in seeing yourself honestly in ways that others might be seeing you. Wow. This is liberating stuff. Not scary. Exciting.

If you are afraid someone might sneak and read your journal, lock it up! I want you to feel very secure about what you are committing to in this journal and to think of it as a friend, because it is! You will want to go back over what you have written time and time again, so you need to save it—at least until this specific exercise related to speaking is complete. That is the reason we undertake this writing exercise—because it is directly related to bringing about the freedom we seek to become eloquent speakers. In this case we are journaling for a specific purpose—although you will inevitably find that it will help you in more diverse ways than just making you a demonstratively effective public speaker.

Before I go any further: NOTE TO MEN—Let me state here at the outset that this is for men as well as women, and in fact it may be more important that men follow this guidance because it is typically easier for us to hide and even bury

these emotional handicaps in our minds. Women have generally been the letter writers and talkers. Men have been more
buttoned up and less verbal or introspective. I know this is a
broad generalization and is not always the case for sure, but I
needed to say it. You may have seen your spouse, partner, or
friend journaling, and it occurs to you that it is a uniquely fem-
inine pursuit—to be so self-reflective. Give it up, man. This
is the time...Besides, no one has to know you are journaling. If you want to get an A in this course, you must do it. It's
required. I am not making you commit to journal for the rest
of your life, although you might become addicted.

Here are just a few examples of some manly and adven-
turesome men in history you may have heard of who have journaled successfully.

Theodore Roosevelt
Thomas Jefferson
Andrew Carnegie
Benjamin Franklin
Meriwether Lewis and William Clark
Captain James Cook
Ralph Waldo Emerson
Sir Edmund Hillary
Bruce Lee
Charles Darwin
Ernest Hemingway
Winston Churchill

For both men and women, this purposeful journaling must
be done on a regular schedule or cycle, and you must commit

to keep at it, at least once a day. You may use an electronic platform or a handwritten one you can fit into your pocket or keep in a desk drawer or bedside table. If you handwrite, choose a journal that is handsome or beautiful. It will add a little bit to your attraction to it. Leather-bound is good for longevity, and since journaling has become popular, good journals with blank or lined pages are easily found in stores or online.

In journal chapter one, begin by listing all the fears you think you might have related to speaking in public. Be specific and descriptive. Identifying these fears, articulating and exposing them, and then looking at them on paper is the best way to begin to belittle them and destroy them. There is something about seeing these anxieties exposed on a piece of paper that makes them seem more trivial, smaller, less significant, daunting, and unresolvable. This is the beginning of separating these fears from us. Seeing them as not permanently in our thinking but outside of it helps immensely with the healing and resolution process.

You may also begin to think of these fears as inhibitors rather than fears. Fears might sound scary to you, and since we want to get rid of them, it might be easier to expect you will be able to conquer inhibitors as mere things that get in your way—in this case in the way of fluid public speaking. Not all your fears will come to mind immediately. Take some time with this. This is a developing list. New ideas about these fears will come to you through interpersonal exchanges, things you read, feelings that get exposed, reactions that come to the surface in your daily routine. Journaling is like sitting with an old friend who already knows everything about you and is a comforting and undemanding presence.

The journal waits for you. It's a patient partner. Dr. James Pennebaker, University of Texas professor and author of *Writing to Heal*, says,

"When we translate an experience into language, we actually make the experience graspable."

I would apply that thought to our situation in this way— "When we translate a fear into a journal entry, we make the fear easier to dispose of."

You might be thinking, "This is interesting, but I do not really have any discernible fears to uncover and deal with. I just want to be a better speaker." I am sure there are plenty of people who would justifiably be able to state that. If that is the case, then do a modest amount of soul searching along the lines I have directed you, and you will still discover things hanging out in your mind that could be inhibitors or could hold you back. Get them into this process, and let's see where it takes you.

Journal Chapter Two: Digging Beneath the Surface

Not all the things that you added to your list in chapter one will be pleasant. After you list your easily perceived fears in chapter one, your next step is this section, where you will ask yourself: what *caused* these fears? This is what I call the "I don't care what my mother thinks of me" section. Make certain you are focused on just this one thing. Match up the fears in the journal's chapter one with the incidents, trauma, life-learning lessons, experiences, schooling and training, and other recollections and memories that you think might have caused these inhibitions.

Your success with this chapter will be in proportion to your honesty. This chapter might cause some uncovering of things you have buried and do not want to bring up again. But remember we are doing this to unleash you from this unwanted master. Ralph Waldo Emerson wrote: *"He has not learned the lesson of life who does not every day surmount a fear."*

This gives us plenty of employment.

In this section I need you to uncover, expose, and list things that may have happened in your youth or adolescence. You need to describe your relationship with your parents and siblings as well as school friends. Were your parents extraordinarily demanding? Did they set the bar high and then judge you for not reaching it? Were you always attempting to win their favor? Were your parents largely absent? Did you have parents? Were they divorced, angry, supportive? Were they too lenient when you craved discipline? It's important to scour the early days, because this is when our speech patterns were developed and set in motion. This is when inhibitions were planted in the conscious and subconscious. This is the time to let go and write. You can go back and make revisions later. You do not have to fear the pain of bringing this all up again. Committing it to your journal will help you know how to cope with inhibitions related to public speaking and other departments of your life. We bring these things up to use them as tools and then move on.

An example of this is my friend Brad, who had tried to conquer his fear of speaking for years. When we started talking about it, I asked him what his mother was like. Although he resisted telling me at first, desiring to protect his mom and be perceived as a good son, he finally relented and told me how much she demanded of him and was excessive in directing everything in his life. She criticized his friends, his clothes, his grades in school, his sports scores, and was generally domineering.

That set up a pattern of Brad trying always to please his mother but never quite meeting her high standards and achieving in her eyes. The result of this carried over and was exhibited whenever Brad had to speak in public. He was unconsciously thinking that his mom was present and criticizing him, which made him halting in his speech pattern and certainly unconfident, because unconsciously he was trying to please her and could not satisfy what she was looking for in him. What a rat race.

He was exhausted by all this but was not really aware of what was causing his anxiety. By merely uncovering and confronting this subconscious tyranny, we were, alongside additional new speaking techniques, able to largely wipe out those bad associations and replace them with confidence. Exposure of this lingering subconscious memory got him two-thirds of the way toward the total destruction of fear's tyrannical hold on him and wiping it out. After all, as an adult, he no longer needed to please his mom. He could now say "Thanks for all the good stuff you gave me, Mom, but I am not listening to you anymore." Asserting this over and over and seeing what a difference it made gave him courage to continue down this path until finally he was completely released from this crippling condition.

In another discussion, this time with Elaine, she shared with me that she had been brought up by foster parents who provided her with a safe home and good education but very little physical or personal affection. She was haunted by the need for affirmation from others and settled into a pattern of trying to please people into giving her compliments. She had such a fear of non-acceptance that she refused to appear at a podium to speak to any sort of group because she just had too much at risk personally.

The more Elaine wrote and journaled about these issues, the more she began to see that they did not have to dominate her life and keep her from accepting her responsibility to help others in ways that might include public speaking. Elaine decided that she would use her life experience as a story to share with her audiences. The more she told the story, the more she could see how it empowered her to help others. She also practiced viewing her experience more impersonally, and eventually it became just a story. It became more important for her to help her audience than to obsess about her past or be trapped in it. At last she was released from the crippling effects of that story and she launched herself all over again.

Yet another woman I worked with, whose name was Janice, was brought up by one parent, and she retained strong feelings of insecurity and anger because of it. This was an unusual case of how fear applied in her situation. She used extreme anger to address her fears, which were basically in the category of fear of inadequacy and of being left alone with little love or help. So in her speeches she was super aggressive. She wanted to win at all cost. This of course drove her audience away from her instead of to her and her message. A wall went right up whenever she started speaking.

It took a lot of convincing and breaking through that hard exterior to get her to even begin to address her fears, but melt it down we did—somewhat. What we accomplished was at least a degree of self-knowledge and reduction in fear that allowed her to become better acquainted with herself, to listen to her voice, and to begin to moderate her presentations based on a decreasing amount of fear and insecurity. Finally, we saw the beginnings of a new person emerge but surely one who will require continuing attention and journaling.

The reasons we dig deeper in this chapter of your journal is not to fret about or try to completely solve the issue you have brought to the surface; indeed, such work is beyond the scope of a book on public speaking. Nevertheless, what we do accomplish is often to make significant strides in minimizing, through exposure, some of the negative features of the past that have emerged as fears and blockages in the present. What individuals who have participated in this type of journaling have reported is that this good, hard work pays dividends far beyond the immediate goal of helping them become masters of fear and better public speakers. It has provided them with the foundation and support to become more fearless and courageous in many aspects of life.

Journal Chapter Three: List the Reasons You Want to Be a Public Speaker

In this chapter of your journal, you start the climb out of the past by focusing on the future. You should feel a freshness in this section, because you are looking toward a new day after facing down the limits of the past that have held you back. Some of your goals might be as simple as learning to communicate better with your family or to advance in your career through accepting jobs that include the responsibility of speaking with groups of people. You should include a wide range of options for yourself and add some goals you might even think are beyond your reach.

This is the beginning of turning your thought and your life toward your audience and away from yourself. Even though most of these goals will be personal ones or career oriented, they are good to identify and solidify as concrete targets. Alongside these targets, begin listing how you think you might accomplish these goals. That might include joining a Toastmasters club, signing up for speech training, or writing an informal talk for your club, church, or community group on a topic that interests you. You do not have to become a whiz overnight or look for an agent to represent you as a professional speaker. A place to start would be to write a speech and deliver it from your script. Start with small but repetitive steps. All speakers, no matter how advanced, need practice to become expert.

There is a big trend in speaking, especially for those who have experienced trauma, addictions, and rehab, to use talk as a personal therapy. This can also be useful in our march toward effective public speaking, but ultimately you have to move past doing this as an extension of therapy and move to a place where you are doing it to be wholly helpful to your audience rather than as a process to expunge your own devils.

Journal Chapter Four: Who Is My Audience and What Is My Impact?

In this final chapter of your journal, you move fully away from yourself to focus outwardly on what you might have to say that the world needs to hear. This is where you begin to link yourself to those who will hear you. This is moving toward what is called audience development. This will put you squarely in a field where you are focused more on the needs of the world, your company, your job, your family, your neighborhood, than yourself. Plan a theoretical speaking tour for yourself. Where would you go, and what would you say? If you cannot come up with anything, ask yourself what your community or your company needs in terms of information, assistance, or some kind of encouragement. If you are not an expert on that topic, make yourself one. Get immersed in the content you want to talk about. These topics might be historical, topical, educational, or inspirational.

I will guarantee you this: if you prepare a talk that is purposeful and informative, and you identify audiences who need to hear your message, you will eventually find yourself in a position where you will receive invitations to speak. Many people polish their speaking skills at public hearings. There are all kinds of these in American cities and towns: public hearings on paving roads, school plans, water sewage plants, and more. People typically have opinions. Go and make yourself heard, in a useful way, not as a nuisance. This is great practice in front of the public. Someone may even hear you and offer an invitation for future speaking platforms.

A couple of years ago I was invited to give the keynote speech at what is called the Lincoln Day Dinner. These are held all around the country to honor our sixteenth president's birthday. I discovered that the woman who was the masterful organizer of the event had put herself in that position simply by the force of her commitment to the life of Lincoln and her commitment to hold one of these dinners in her community. She was not a trained speaker, but she became so passionate about this subject and event that she lost all inhibitions and fears and became the master of ceremonies for the whole evening, an event that was enjoyed by many people. That is one of the great things about America. Many of the things we can think up we can do. For speaking in public it all starts with lifting your own self-imposed limitations. Many Americans consider themselves self-made. Each of us has the individual opportunity to craft a new purpose in life, and each new day provides the platform.

When you complete the fourth chapter of your journal, do not put it aside. Keep it active. Life is a series of progressions someone has called "repeating and defeating, repeating and defeating." Keep active in this journal and add to it. It will keep on helping you. Perhaps one day you will give a speech about what you have written in your journal.

Physical Tactics to Control Fear

Controlling fear is not the same as mastering it. Nonetheless anything helps when nervousness threatens to take over. Here are a few tips.

1. Make absolutely certain you have complete confidence in the content of your speech and that there are no unforced errors in it. If you think to yourself: "I know my speech is well written and has solid content," this alone will calm fears and jitters.

2. Practice! Then practice again. Get comfortable with delivering the content. This should help. Be on time for the speech! On the way to the venue play your favorite upbeat music. Sing along!

3. Always ask for a podium from which you can present. It helps to hide yourself a little bit and not to be exposed to the audience so completely and threateningly. Rest your hands on the podium for additional comfort.

4. If you think you might need eyeglasses to get through your speech, make sure you have them in your pocket. If you wear contact lenses, carry an extra pair. Also carry a handkerchief and any other personal items you need. Wear clothing that is warm enough but not too hot and not too tight to cause you to think about your body. Wear comfortable shoes.

5. Before your speech use the bathroom. Always drink room-temperature water—before and not during. Cold or ice water constricts the vocal cords. Avoid it. This way you can always say to yourself that you have taken care of these physical needs and they do not need to bother you anymore.

6. If you need to write out every word of your lecture to calm yourself, then do so. There is nothing wrong with this, especially if it will make you feel secure. I have also seen an effective little device of language work miracles. I have heard speakers say to an audience, "Please bear with me this morning as I feel a little nervous sharing this with you.

I will try my best." This charming little personal admission has drawn audiences up close and resulted in an immediate dissolution of the fourth wall. It has to be done with utter and complete genuineness. If you feel this way in your heart, you can verbalize it this way, and it will work.

7. Most important, get yourself enthused about the content of your speech. Get really excited about it, even if you are delivering bad news, so much so that you forget you have persistent fears or anxiety. Lose any self-consciousness through immersion in the text, the ideas, the inspiration, and its gift to the audience. You know you have done your best in all your preparation. Now, let it go.

Mental Strategies to Conquer Fear

There are many paths to fully conquering fear related to speaking. So far, I have given you some practical tools. On a deeper level, ridding yourself of an underlying and persistent fear may be a lifelong adventure, and yet it does not have to disturb and limit your life's work as a speaker.

Some individuals have turned to faith to resolve fear, some meditation, some raw human courage. Dr. Martin Luther King Jr. devoted an early, hour-long sermon to this subject. It was called "The Conquest of Fear" and was delivered on August 20, 1950, when he was helping his father pastor at Ebenzer Baptist Church, and is worth reading in its entirety. In it he powerfully professed his belief that "fear can only be

Dr. King, the master of soaring rhetoric, used storytelling to drive home a meaningful lesson.

destroyed through faith." He then added this picturesque and poignant saying which he repeated from an old colloquial truism, "Fear knocked at the door. Faith answered. There was no one there." He also reminded the audience throughout his lengthy and inspired sermon of the statement from the Bible, "Perfect love casteth out fear," and he highlighted how this truth could be used to defeat many aspects of fear from global crisis to individual fear for one's life, as he himself had to confront time and time again.

Our fears of public speaking would pale in comparison to all the fears Dr. King had to face, and yet we can apply his guidance in our job to resolve fear associated with standing before an audience. After considering different ways to defeat fear, we can turn our focus with a mighty effort to our audience and to our content to the degree that we forget about ourselves, our nerves, distractions, insecurities, and troubles. That is the ultimate way to conquer fear in speaking.

Shifting the weight of our thought outward to focus on the audience and to what they seek and to be completely absorbed in the content and delivery will put you in a position of power over the enemy of fear. When you do this consistently over a period of several speeches, you will become immune to the fear, and your talks will become calm and confident because you are becoming successful and your audiences are rewarding you with new confidence. This is you loving your message, your audience, and becoming at one with them, canceling the division that fear can cause.

CHAPTER FIVE

Building a Bridge to Your Audience

Always recognize the humanity of your audience.

Dr. David Lubin, art historian and
lecturer, Wake Forest University

Bringing Down the Fourth Wall

Earlier in this book you have read references to the fourth wall. Now we will focus on what it is and how you will bring it down.

As one of their first lessons stage actors are taught about the fourth wall. As a speaker or presenter you need to know about it as well. Understanding it and dealing effectively with it can make or break a success for you on stage or in broadcast and video as well. This law comes into play when you are "facing" any audience and it is a useful and instructive metaphor for the student of oratory.

When you are on a stage, it's plain to identify and see the three physical walls, the ones to your left and right and the one behind you. What you may not see with your eyes is the wall in front of you. This is the barrier you are left to bring down though your own performance and your own authentic force of personality and ability to connect with the audience in front of you. No one else can do this work for you. This is obviously not a physical barrier but rather a mental one, and it is your job to tear it down and clear out the remaining debris so you can then start building a bridge to your audience over which you will travel to them and they to you, creating a fruitful and beneficial interactive relationship.

This theoretical wall is constructed of some of these seven building elements that might keep the performer and audience separated.

1. Skepticism
2. Boredom
3. Prejudice
4. Inattentiveness
5. Nervousness
6. Closemindedness
7. Resistance to new ideas or change

These elements, if not brought down, can create an impenetrable separation between you and your audience. If this wall persists, it is almost impossible to build the bridge needed to send your vital message into the ears, hearts, and minds of the audience. Actors know when they have connected with their audience, and it is their first and primary job to do so once the curtain goes up. Think about it the next time you are at the theater or even attending a musical concert. Sometimes it works and sometimes not. It is a feeling that you have as an audience member, and you will know if the actor or the musician has really reached you, moved you, inspired you, changed you in some way. It might even be difficult for the audience to describe this feeling in words. The way the audience feels about a performer can make or break the outcome. All the responsibility to accomplish this falls on the shoulders of the presenter. That is why we focus on developing this skill.

Here are seven keys to help you bring down this wall and get through to and "reach" your audience.

1. Before you even arrive at your speech destination, think about your talk with gratitude and expectation that something good is going to result from your effort.

2. Clear away any of your own doubt about your success.

3. Reaffirm to yourself how vital your message really is and how confident you are in the content.

4. Greet the audience with open arms and an open thought. No judgment or criticism allowed. Leave that at the "stage door."

5. Maintain the attitude that the audience before you is your partner.

6. Thank them before you even appear on stage, for attending and for being receptive to your message.

7. Begin with a smile, and share how happy you are about this opportunity to spend time with them, and mention their generosity in having come to hear you.

Now stop and create your own list. Think of what could contribute to a fourth wall of division for you when you face an audience. Then make a list of the qualities and skills you could apply to bring down this wall.

Here are some stories and examples of how people have brought down this wall.

When I accompanied Nancy Reagan on one of her first significant trips to visit a major residential drug abuse treatment and rehabilitation center, our plan was to attend a graduation program where the residents learned whether or not they had "earned," through being "clean," the right to return home to live with their parents. As the evening progressed, the emotional level increased in the massive gymnasium filled with hundreds of nervous kids and emotional parents. It became obvious that the remarks officially prepared for the first lady on typed five-by-eight-inch index cards wouldn't even begin to be appropriate given all that the assembled crowd had been through in the course of the evening so they were thrown out. After all even the Secret Service agents and the traveling press corps members were crying.

It was then, when called upon, that the first lady was handed a microphone and went to the center of the cavernous fieldhouse. She delivered the most moving, sincere, and memorable speech of her eight years in the White House. There was no second-guessing. These extemporaneous remarks had to come directly from her heart, as the audience and the situation demanded. No one could do this for her. No typed index cards would suffice. She dug deeply to find the words. And yes, she shed tears during her presentation, but everyone knew they were real—because everyone in the audience felt the

same way. This was the ultimate way to bring down any separation between her and the audience. She talked a lot about
love, and that is always the most powerful uniter—if expressed
genuinely. The press corps was puzzled. Was this the same
Nancy Reagan they, the journalists, had excoriated for having
no heart? That was the night they began to see her somewhat
differently. For any speaker there may be these rare times
when prepared remarks are simply not appropriate.

I would say that when we arrived at the event site that evening, even though Mrs. Reagan was welcomed, there was a wall
of speculation about her being there. This made up the fourth
wall—the doubt that she was genuine and more than just a
figurehead pulling off a public relations ploy. Ultimately she
brought down more than one wall that evening. She brought
down a wall between her and the reporters who observed her
as well as the audience who felt it. It was a powerful evening
and even a lesson for her which gave her more confidence in
delivering the many speeches she was required to undertake
in the years following that trip. During her tenure she never
became a comfortable or exceptional public speaker but the
experience of that night showed her a way to effectively reach
an audience. After this experience I noticed at various stops
throughout the years that young people, especially, made an
easy connection with her and one time even hoisted her on
their shoulders and carried her around and celebrated her for
her work in drug remediation as well as her vulnerability.

I will never forget attending a funeral at a large inner-city
church. The service was in honor of a young boy, the son of an
employee at our church, who had been gunned down on an
inner-city street by an off-duty policeman and had died at the

hospital that same night. I had received a call in the middle of the night from his inconsolable father about this incident. Although this was not my own church or congregation and there was a printed program with designated speakers from the community, including the mayor, I sat there agonizing about the need for someone from our own church to make remarks. Finally, I stood and asked if I could approach the altar where the mourners were deep in sadness and sorrow at the bloodshed and shocking loss of life.

Although I had not prepared one word of remarks, I knew I had to dig deeply into my own heart for something to say. What came out of my mouth was simply to tell the congregation about support they had from our church and the love we had for this man and his son. Then I thought of a more eloquent man than I and quoted from the sermon found in the Book of Revelation in which St. John sees an end to all pain, suffering, and crying. This is what occurred to me to share at that moment in that church in front of an audience I did not know. Humble as these remarks were, they illustrated what any speaker might be called upon to do when a written speech is not enough. The impetus comes from understanding the need of the audience and responding to it in the best way you can. It may not be grand, but if spoken from the heart, it will be acceptable to those who have hearts. I think handling my remarks this way brought down any fourth wall of separation between two congregations of completely different racial makeup.

These examples of flexibility and responsiveness to an audience and their success all depended in one way or another on understanding the dynamics of the audience. When thinking about a group of people assembled to listen to a speech, it is important not to think of the group as a passive gathering. Any gathering of people for the purpose of listening to a message represents many differing dispositions, emotions, points of view—all brought together for a program they either desire to attend or were required to.

Many speakers who are on the road giving speeches all the time may second-guess their audiences, thinking them to be sometimes unresponsive and passive. Understanding the texture of the crowd, that some are coming dog-tired from work or childcare and want to be anywhere but your speech, that some are earning course credit or certification to listen to you, might help you relate to the audience, understand them, have compassion and respect them for being there and spending their time with you.

Who Is Your Audience?

During the Reagan years I found myself one day, along with a team of White House advance office team members, on a helicopter loaned to us by the chancellor of Germany. We were flying blind in the Bavarian Alps in the middle of dense clouds and riding like a roller coaster dipping to treetop level and back up again, flying over a dense green forest. Frankly, we thought we were destined to crash and started talking about the best way to survive a helicopter dive into the treetops below. We even discussed the headlines that would appear the next morning about the White House staff's disappearance in this remote mountainous region. The pilots didn't appear worried, but we were. After what seemed like an eternity, we found a clearing and landed. Thanks to the competency of our German flight engineers and an early version of GPS, we had arrived safely at our precise destination, a thirteenth-century castle where we wanted the president to make a major speech about German reunification.

Hambach Castle, we learned, was the site of the historic 1832 Festival of Democracy and ever since then has been linked to the early and sustained democracy movement in Germany. Though this impressive structure dated back to late Roman times and had been destroyed in several fires and conflicts, it had been rebuilt and had hosted many meetings, including an annual youth encampment to talk about and celebrate democratic principles. This was a perfect venue for Reagan, who was an unapologetic evangelist for democracy and freedom, and who readily spoke about it everywhere he was invited—and even some places where he was not.

When we returned in May with the president, it was a considerably warmer and cloudless day, and while we again landed by chopper, it was without any of the threatening turbulence we had encountered on our advance trip. As we landed this time we observed an even more impressive site. Thousands of young people were gathered on the grassy areas surrounding the ancient fortification—all invited there to hear the American president—while attending the programs focused on government and leadership. As Reagan took his place on the custom-built dais, I plunged into the crowd to get a feel for their reaction to what the president would say. I tried to blend in as best as was possible, and that was not too difficult as I was not much older than these college students. For that afternoon I wanted to be one of them just waiting for the major remarks of the day.

In retrospect this was an ideal way to understand a crowd. I was a small part of planning this event, and now I was officially a part of the audience. I wanted to listen and to observe, just like the others assembled there that day, to judge their reaction and rub shoulders with them. The president gave perhaps, to me, his most inspired invocation that day, challenging these young people to dedicate themselves to the cause of freedom and reunification—for Germany's sake and theirs. He did his usual masterful verbal recounting of the good in German history, reminding the audience of their vast legacy, and then enjoined them to rise to the prospect of their promising future, as free and unified people.

For an hour or so, I was the audience, and before I had to race back to the departure point for embarkation or lose my place in the staff helicopter, I turned to look at the crowd I had just been a part of. I felt the energy there that day, and I saw the approving faces and multiple interruptions for applause. It was a day among so many remarkable Reagan days I will never forget. It was also a perfect study of what one type of audience might be, what they looked like and how they responded. While the outdoor audience was large, Reagan's message was personal. I studied the reaction from the audience. They were drawn in to it because it had something for them and it was tailored precisely to their concerns, hopes, and to their own future. It was a message that needed to be delivered to an audience that already shared the concerns addressed on that historic site.

Most of us will never be a speaker to crowds like presidents or heads of state who have listeners that number in the thousands. Or like Pope John Paul II, who delivered a mass for unexpected millions who greeted him upon his triumphant and daring 1979 return to Poland, the country of his birth and early life. In ways, however, any audience, despite its size, includes similar features to be knowledgeable about. At times even an intimate audience of a dozen could seem more profitable and rewarding than thousands or the millions waiting for the pontiff in Warsaw.

I remember one evening driving from Washington, DC, to Annapolis, Maryland, where I had accepted an invitation to speak at a municipal public library. On our one-hour drive east we wondered if this would be worth our time or if anyone would even show up. When we arrived, the librarians were warm and welcoming, but there was no evidence there would be many in the audience. Then something interesting happened. The crowd began to arrive, and the librarians had to search for more chairs. Soon it was the largest crowd they had ever seen in that space.

As I surveyed the gathering crowd, I decided to attempt a different approach rather than launching right into my talk. I decided to reach out to the audience first. This was not my usual practice or the way I suggest anyone to begin a talk. In this case, even though the crowd had grown to be a good size, it seemed intimate and people sort of crowded in. So I adapted my talk to the audience.

To start us off, I asked people to voluntarily retell some of their own personal experiences related to the topic of the evening. What followed was a genuine sharing of inspiring stories that lasted for about twenty minutes. It drew us up close, as a group, like family who had just shared some intimate experiences. You could feel a special friendship among people who mostly did not know one another. That was an audience that impressed me for the warmth they brought with them, which I felt was even more than I had brought to the occasion. Audiences can surprise you on an occasion like that and contribute to the outcome of an event in a memorable way. It was a lesson for me not to judge an audience too harshly and to be open to what any group might bring to the talk, in terms of richness of experience and talent of their own. Maintaining an attitude of appreciation and gratitude for your audience will unquestionably be felt by them. For any presentation, no matter how small or large, the talk and the audience joining in a compact and looking for something of import to happen is the most desirable goal. Remember as a speaker, you need an audience of some kind to complete the experience. It's a joint-venture operation or event.

On another, more recent drive to Annapolis, I was traveling there to speak to a very small group of midshipmen at the Naval Academy. My topic was the role of intuition in military leadership. We met over dinner at the Navy Mess. Because of the intimacy of the group, I was able to amend my usual way of speaking and reach out with a few ideas and then let my hosts, who were the audience, and the cadets ask questions and share their experiences about military life and leadership. Again, this was an adaptive and interactive approach to a small gathering that was a success. Both of these experiences were unplanned. As a speaker you learn to watch for these opportunities to help make something remarkable happen. Its requires a knowledge of your content, a knowledge of your audience, and flexibility about how to most effectively bring the two together. This is your responsibility as a speaker.

Getting Acquainted with the Audience

Here are four points to take into consideration when thinking about your audience and preparing your speech. I have seen speakers ignorantly mount the podium and begin a prepared speech without any reference to what city they are in or to incidents that might have affected how people feel about being there to listen at that moment. What a lost opportunity to build a bridge to the audience.

1. Always conduct a little research prior to arriving or in the moments before you are introduced. Ask your host to describe the attendees, what they might be looking to gain from your speech, their age groups, education level, anything else about them that would be pertinent to your topic or revealing of their state of mind. At one time I spoke in Ann Arbor, Michigan, home to the University of Michigan. Although I had foolishly expected most of the audience to represent the student population and planned my remarks for that type of audience, I learned that there is a large retirement community in Ann Arbor, which was generously represented there, and that surprised me somewhat as I

looked out across the auditorium. I had to do some quick rearranging of my remarks to be inclusive of everyone there.

2. Do a little research on the town or location where the audience is coming from. Have you visited there before? Is it totally new to you? Is it an urban location faced with tension and crime? A retirement community? A sports-oriented community with a major sports franchise that transfixes a big segment of the population during the season? It might be good to learn if the home team is having a winning season or not. It is amazing how something like this will immediately win your audience to your side. Their reaction might be "Now that is a woman I really want to listen to. She gets it—understands where we are coming from and what really excites (or disturbs) us." If people like what you have said about them or their town or their commitment to something, you will see them glance at the people around them affirmatively and typically with smiles. They will appreciate that you went the extra mile to learn more about them and, as a result, may be better listeners.

3. Determine if there have been any recent news-making or dramatic events in the area. New growth, new jobs, store closings? Is it a tech center, college town, industrial giant, declining in population? Find out about the environment you are entering by, at a minimum, Googling it. At one time I was invited to speak in a city and a corporate headquarters where I thought my remarks might be met with a hostile response. My homework on the area and on my host was inadequate

and not dependable. Although I was prepared to bolster my defenses against possible opposition, the crowd could not have been more friendly. I was totally incorrect about how I approached them, and I felt bad that I had not gone deeper to learn more about the audience I would be addressing from the senior management at the firm hosting me.

4. If your speech is not in the country where you live or you are a giving a speech that will require simultaneous translation, be sure your remarks have been vetted by people who know and understand the culture and nuances of that language. The last thing you want is to have your remarks misunderstood. At one time I was invited on a goodwill speaking tour throughout Austria. I visited towns that represented varied interests, history, and culture within the same country. Fortunately for me, my host was an official from the country's Chamber of Commerce, and everywhere we went I was fully briefed on the economic and cultural history of the area. This provided me with immediate topics for conversation, including some I could weave into my prepared remarks. Some speakers may have to do this work for themselves, but it may pay off in an invitation to return and speak again.

Manipulating or Motivating Your Audience

Today, an audience is not defined exclusively as a group of people assembled in a physical space for the purpose of hearing someone speak on a topic. An audience might be one person listening to you on a podcast, webinar, blog, Skype, Zoom, YouTube, LinkedIn, an infomercial, or a social media post. It might be a single individual or a large group of individuals who are influenced by what you say, and you may never see or know who the audience is. Influencers, like speakers, also have audiences—people who follow a lifestyle or advice and who may choose to follow the lead, direction, or opinions of these individuals. The audience might be a targeted and well-profiled and vetted group of people who respond to an advertising campaign for a product or a politician. As a speaker you might also refer to an audience as those listening to you if you are appearing on a talk or interview show broadcast in one of many formats on TV and on other platforms.

When it comes to influencing or advertising, the audience could become an economic or political target or opportunity. A significant amount of research typically goes into segmenting and identifying the type of audience that will produce the highest result, measured by the audience response. The response could be purchasing something as a result of seeing a product placement in a film, print, or TV ad, or even because a speaker has used key phrases or words that trigger a reaction. The outcome for the audience might be influencing them to become active in a campaign or voting for an individual or cause. It might also be convincing them to take specific action because of the audience-targeted advertising or outreach.

For example, if you attend a talk by a noted chef or food magazine critic, you might find yourself leaving the talk hungry. If you listen to a noted art curator or designer, you may go home and throw out all your old furniture or artwork and want to start all over again. In advertising, the better the audience is defined and targeted relative to the product, the higher the percentage of response and the more successful the campaign. While advertising is designed to manipulate an audience, speakers who are considered leading authorities on a topic can be manipulative as well.

While the orator's stock-in-trade is typically practicing the art of rhetoric or persuasion on topics the audience voluntarily selects to attend, the orator may also practice subtle manipulation where an audience has not given their permission. Attempting to move the listener to the speaker's point of view may be a part of the speaker's motivation and purpose in giving a speech. While some speeches may have that result, most speakers are not insistent that the listening audience adopt their proposals. If they are, it seems reasonable that they provide some sort of disclosure such as "I am going to speak to you about the value of bonds in today's investment climate, and I want you to know that I also sell bonds."

Some speeches are given on controversial topics and demand that the audience consider a point of view in comparison to their own. A good example was a speech I attended recently on sharks. The learned, reasonable, and academically trained speaker, who also showed a dramatic and emotional film graphically illustrating how millions of sharks are killed each year by line fishing, was compelling and impressive. I found the talk more informative than demanding of me that I adopt the point of view of the speaker.

To me this was an ideal type of advocacy. It did have its impact on me, because I left that program wanting to take action against shark poaching—even though the speaker did not specifically ask me to do that. For me that is the most effective way to use words (and pictures) to let the listener make his own determination after considering the factual and biased or unbiased material presented. Sometimes, however, speakers present their point of view and supporting evidence and then pointedly or even forcefully ask the audience to become activists on an issue or even to make financial contributions.

A public speaker as a manipulator, rather than solely an informer or educator, may speak for positive or negative purposes in political contexts or related to commerce, science, or some other topic. Manipulation as a process can be used to promote the common good or to destroy it. Manipulation can employ a mesmerizing crowd psychology to lead people to take action or make people think they want something. The speaker might use mood-shifting language or music to make people think that they desire a specific outcome when they may be allowing the speaker to control their thoughts through persuasion, irrationality, suggestion, or contagion.

Depending on the authority of the speaker and their ability to motivate, ideas might be transferred to the minds of audience to even make them think they have thought of these ideas themselves and have not been instructed or even educated or informed by someone else. The message might then become separated from the messenger, organizer, or speaker. Political movements can be described in this way, such as seen in the 2019 Hong Kong, Venezuelan, Turkish, Puerto Rican, and other uprisings and protests. The objective and attendant skill to win an audience are always required by the organizers.

Even in this case of political gamesmanship, focusing and motivating an audience is key to bringing their influence to bear on the political issues being discussed in the presentation.

In these more acute and high-stakes situations, the same rules of effective public speaking pertain. As always, the primary goal is to know your audience and make them feel your presentation warrants their support and their trust in your authority.

One of the greatest examples of political manipulation for positive good through a speech, with potentially life-saving results, was Churchill's speech delivered to Parliament and designed to bolster and raise the courage of the British people and to encourage them to fight on and to give them the moral support they needed. Delivered on June 4, 1940, with such gravity and earnestness, it was said that Churchill was actually encouraging himself with the words he spoke, which is something Reagan often did as well with his remarks. It reached the hearts and minds of everyone who heard it and helped to galvanize the resolve for the work ahead. In it he makes this call:

We shall defend our Island, whatever the cost may be, we shall fight on the beaches, we shall fight on the landing grounds, we shall fight in the fields and in the streets, we shall fight in the hills; we shall never surrender.

It is even more frightening to know that at the time this speech was given, there was actually talk of surrender, and of course had Great Britain done that, western civilization would have taken a distinctly different course. Churchill's speeches helped turn the tide of a nation's resolve and commitment, which could be compared to other members of the allied nations, such as France and Belgium, who lacked a public

Churchill used his voice to call a nation to victory and to comfort it in misery.

speaker and leader like Churchill who was able to use the gift of oratory to help mobilize a nation and to sustain its morale.

In fact the British Broadcasting Corporation grew to achieve its finest hours during World War II when it expanded its broadcast reach to the heart of Europe for several reasons, including for the broadcast of Churchill's speeches—sent out to encourage all the people of a free Europe and listened to even by some in Germany and Italy who secretly hoped, prayed, and worked for an Allied victory. Thousands listened, many endangering themselves, to hear his voice bring encouragement across Europe.

Another example of political manipulation for the common good is the John F. Kennedy inaugural address of January 20, 1961. It was delivered from the East Front of the Capitol in freezing conditions. In it, the youngest man ever elected president calls a nation to duty and courage. His remarks, of course, included this historic and often repeated line:

> *And so, my fellow Americans: Ask not what your country can do for you—ask what you can do for your country.*

The design of that statement was to mobilize millions, just as Churchill had in more dire circumstances, to fight for equality and achieve the greatness that was a part of America's destiny.

Are You Separate from Your Audience?

Your primary job as an orator is to elicit a response from your audience. This may be achieved through the effective delivery of information, enlightenment, education, inspiration, motivation, or entertainment. The way your audience processes what you say in their own minds is what matters. The way you form your words and your individual, personal credibility are being processed by the listeners, unless they have tuned out, are checking their phones, or are napping—which could be the case in any audience today. You may be standing in front of them a few yards away, possibly on an elevated podium or stage, but the distance from your words and concepts to their consciousness is not measured in feet or yards; it is instantaneous and does not necessarily require a physical measurement. It is your thought to their thought—conveyed partly through sound waves but also though nonverbal messaging.

Have you ever had the experience or heard of someone explaining, "This morning I was thinking of Jake, and lo and behold he called on my cell phone ten minutes later! I never even had to reach out to him." Research on this type of nonverbal communication has only scratched the surface and yet is essential for the public speaker to understand in knowing how to reach the audience. If you are in tune with your subject matter and your audience at the same time and are deeply immersed in and appreciative of both, you can make the meaning of what you are saying more acute and real for the listener. On the other hand, if you are tepid about your subject matter and uninterested in the audience, the thought waves will not connect. Treating your audience with a genuine level of conviction and interest, you will get positive feedback, and they will get the meaning of your message.

I will share with you how this has worked for me as a listener in an audience. My guess is that you have experienced this as well. Recently I was focused intently on a lecture. I was attentive but not really expecting to take away much inspiration I could use. Then the speaker said something in a unique way, emphasizing words I had heard before but now in a different configuration and tone. As a result the meaning hit me in a way I had never thought of before. It set off a whole new way of looking at something I was dealing with in my business. Now, the speaker didn't do anything to customize his speech for me or even look me directly in the eye, or stop and explain his point, but he was obviously thinking about this point in a way that he also felt it was important. That communicated itself to me without any detailed explanation. The inspiration in his mind came into my life, and I was the beneficiary.

He went right on with his responsibility to the whole audience, and yet I was left there in my seat with a whole new view—and one that was useful to me. Every individual in the audience is bringing a wholly unique set of perspectives and life experiences to your talk. If your desire as a speaker is to give something of value—even life-transforming—it can happen. As a speaker you should always be open to what I call "the unplanned enlightenment that can happen in the room spontaneously." Listeners can feel new points of view, revelations, or just satisfaction from what you say. That is what I always strive for as a speaker.

Another example for me comes from the talks I have given about President Reagan. People may be coming to these talks wanting to hear the details of his life and my experiences with him, but they also might have a deeper need to hear how he achieved his highly regarded leadership style. In my talks we focus on his character and faith. Many people are learning about these aspects of this character for the first time. At a few of these talks I have been inspired to ask if the group would like to sing one of Reagan's favorite church hymns. I have never had any audience turn me down on this, and I can also report that when I end the talk this way and say good night to the crowd, most have tears in their eyes. This happens, of course, because they have been moved in some way by this experience. I did not make them cry. They were moved emotionally by how the music and the ideas we shared touched their own hearts. If you desire to provide inspiration or are open to new ideas developing at your talks, you should think of yourself as a sponsor of new ideas and opportunity for reflection and discovery that may reach the hearts of the people in the audience.

Another example of how new ideas can be generated by a talk is from the quarterly presentations I attend hosted by a social impact business incubator based in Washington, DC. When I listen to these remarkably articulate inventors give their talks, which are all based on their life stories, not only am I moved by their remarkable commitment to create a better world, but their energy and inventiveness are contagious for me. Right while they are presenting and I am listening, I may get a brand-new idea about an approach to a business problem I have been dealing with.

This is a fertile environment with ideas bouncing around the room like popcorn. It's a creative environment. That is why I try never to miss one of these programs. This also illustrates the best kind of connection between speaker and audience. There is so much earnestness and authenticity illustrated by the stories of their own suffering and rise out of it that it makes you rise up and be inspired as well. I am sure I am not the only person in the audience who feels this way, because I have spoken with others about it. I would not call this inspiration so much as I would describe it as a way "to elevate," which is one word my friend and Rhodes Scholar, author, TV personality, and leader Wes Moore adopted and shared with me as his life's credo and the way he concludes every email he writes: ELEVATE! In a way that should be the goal for every speech, talk, or remarks we deliver and every webinar and podcast we present.

CHAPTER SIX

Crossing the Bridge to Your Audience

Conveying Your Content to Its Intended Recipients

Is physical distance a barrier for effective communication or speech? Of course, physical barriers could be walls, structures, barricades. But let's assume you and your audience are in the same room or same space, which might be a conference room, office, or stadium. Let's also assume that your remarks might be broadcast over a virtual network or web-based platform. We have just used the examples of Churchill being heard by people throughout Europe, hiding in their homes and huddling around the radio, and John F. Kennedy standing with his top hat and morning coat in the freezing cold delivering his first and only inaugural address in front of a distinguished group of invitees at the Capitol and yet heard throughout the world as it was the first presidential inauguration televised in color.

These are examples of crossing the bridge that speakers have used in reaching their audiences. That would be a bridge of confidence and trust in the veracity of the speaker and the poignancy and power of the content. That would mean a willingness on the part of the audience to listen to you and your message. You have worked hard to build the bridge to them. Now what could hamper that delivery, and conversely what could make it successful?

Physical and mental barriers to receiving your message, thrown up or experienced by the audience, might include the following elements:

1. **A poor sound or amplification system or poor acoustics.** In any crowd there will be people who suffer hearing loss. Even people who wear hearing aids may not hear the same quality of sound or might be reticent to turn up the volume on their personal devices because of possible feedback from the amplification system in the hall. Always be aware of this barrier, and make certain you are speaking in a strong, clear voice that can be heard. Maintain the attitude that your message is important and worth being heard.

2. **Poor sight lines or lighting that keeps the audience from seeing you.** If there is an overflow crowd or additional rooms where the audience will access you via closed-circuit television feed, you can be sure that your effectiveness in those rooms will be only a percentage of what you can achieve with the audience with you in the room with you, the presenter. If the dais or stage is dark and not properly

lit, this is also a barrier. People can generally hear better if they can see you. I have seen poor stage lighting or none at all as the most common problem in halls where people make presentations. The stage or podium should always be in a stronger light than the audience. This is also critical for all video production.

3. **Native language barriers.** If you are not speaking in your native language or if you have simultaneous translators, you may need to account for that and have patience with an audience that would probably like to hear you but cannot fully process what you are saying. They might also not process some words that you might be using colloquially. Even if you are speaking in your native language, it is also possible that, if you speak with unusual inflections or a regional accent, this might slow down the processing of your message by the audience. The best you can do is to be aware of these barriers and try to compensate for them by explaining what you bring to the podium in terms of language and talk a little about where you were brought up. This will add some personality, charm, and warmth that may help endear you to the audience instead of frustrating them.

4. **Late to arrive or begin.** Audiences typically have little patience with speakers who arrive late or begin their speeches after the advertised time. Their justifiable point of view is that they got there on time, and you should as well. In the rare case that you do arrive late, make certain

you apologize and give a full and credible explanation and ask for their understanding. You will have to re-earn their trust once you do get underway. On the flip side, if there has been a weather incident or bad traffic that keeps your audience from attending on time, it would be gracious of you to suggest to those who have arrived that you wait to start until a larger crowd has been able to assemble. This is just another way to create a bond with the audience. Candor and honesty will always win the day.

5. **A slide show or PowerPoint.** With some exceptions we now live in a post-PowerPoint era. While slides or videos can be inspiring or provide useful data, they may sap the energy from what you are saying. For about a decade, speakers thought that reading the copy on a set of slides constituted a speech—that is, until audiences started not to buy it and just requested copies of the slides be sent to them and ditched their attendance at the speech. As a convener of panel and roundtable discussions, both of which I am seriously opposed to as effective formats to convey information, I let it be known among my panelists that no PowerPoint presentations would be allowed. Finally, most conference organizers banned them as well. The only time I feel slides might be justified would be when you are lecturing about art, travel, or real estate, all of which require visuals to illustrate your points.

6. **Personal bias.** It is sad to say, but speakers should not be naïve about the fact that some in your audience may

have political, cultural, racial, sexual, age, or educational biases that keep them from listening to you and receiving your message. You might say, "Then, why did they choose to attend my talk?" Sometimes attendance at speeches might be required by an employer, even for professional licensing credit, and sometimes people may just be curious. The best way to deal with possible prejudice is to put on your most sincere and authentic presentation with confidence and authority but without any feeling of personal threat on your part. You are not there to make someone believe you but to present your material honestly and convincingly. Who knows? The way a listener enters the hall may not be the same way they exit. You could show them there is no need for prejudicial thinking. Never play defense. Never apologize but always be humble and gracious. Arrogance and superiority will never win the day with any audience.

7. **Protestors and disruptors.** Unless you are a politician, it is rare that an invited speaker would encounter protests from the audience. Protestors, however, are becoming more prevalent on college campuses where invited guests sometimes offer ideas opposed to views held by the students and faculty. I have also attended corporate shareholder meetings where the officers and presenters have been interrupted by shareholders who want to challenge a point of governance or management. Evelyn Y. Davis, a Dutch native and Holocaust survivor, created the role of

corporate gadfly by making herself the nemesis of more than eighty corporate CEOs and chairmen. She reigned in this controversial role for fifty years, until her death in 2018. She gained access to these meetings by purchasing shares of the company's stock and then attending mostly to heckle the senior management.

No one has emerged to fill her precise role but, following her lead, some corporate activists have challenged management at shareholder meetings, often in a more sophisticated way and with the intent to influence or to gain control of the company through changes to the board makeup. In general, most corporate leaders handle these types of interruptions poorly and lack the kind of training that should be a priority for them.

While there is really no manual or perfect model for how to handle protestors who interrupt your speech, here are a few pointers on how to do it.

- *Be thoroughly briefed* on any possibility of a protest demonstration. Such groups are often required to obtain a municipal license for their activities, so there's no valid reason not to be prepared. Do not be caught off-guard. There are many ways to plan for the interruption. You should not only prepare for this but drill for how it will be handled.

- *Do not engage* in any way to escalate the confrontation if one should occur. This passive approach may deny the protestors their very objective. Their strategy is to use the assembled crowd and hold them hostage to listen to them instead of you. Remember any protest is the responsibility of your host organization and not you. You are the guest and typically the accidental target. Remember you are strong and they are weak. You have been invited, they have not.

- *If you personally are the target of a protest, you may need to take more responsibility,* while remaining in control and nonconfrontational. This is not the time to try to win an argument with them. They may be in the wrong and you in the right, but this is not the time to prove it. You might offer them an opportunity to meet afterward to have a serious and respectful conversation. Above all, you want to remain the winner in the immediate situation and not enlarge the controversy and make a bigger story out of it.

- *Even though you have been invited to be there, and they have not, you need to remember that our nation is built on the protection of free speech and assembly.* While these people may actually be intruders on private property, it is good to recognize and keep the perspective that they are using your audience as an opportunity to communicate their views. Although you should always be vigilant about security, you should maintain a personally nonthreatening physical posture. It might be hard to do this, especially if you are the target of threatening language, but you must remain nonconfrontational. The reason this is important is that protests can escalate into violence that could hurt people.

- Assuming you are in place because you have been invited to speak on a specific subject, you might *remain focused on delivering your speech* and talk through the disturbance or ask the audience to remain calm until the intruders have been ushered out by security.

Working in politics, as I did, you become more accustomed to protests and interrupters. The biggest effort is made on the side of avoiding a collision of viewpoints, because that becomes the news story and drowns out the real purpose of the event as planned. If you have Secret Service protection, or even private security, you can rest a great deal of authority with them because they are trained to protect you, and they also know the legal ramifications of controlling interruptions. It is true that some individuals play by a different book of rules. They want to control a message through disruption and chaos. It is good to recognize this and also to immediately call for security or police protection if you feel personally threatened in any way. News media thrives on controversy and disruptors know this. Being prepared is the only way to deal with or manage these situations. Know where the exits are for any room in which you are speaking.

I remember numerous occasions when, traveling with the Reagans, the motorcade drove directly into and through protests and demonstrations. One time when we were in London a group of women had obtained a license to protest and to throw bottles of blood on us. It was a tough decision, in consultation with the Secret Service, as to whether to proceed with the event or cancel it. We did proceed, exercising all caution, and thankfully the approved demonstration never materialized.

On one memorable trip to Portugal when the president was speaking to the Portuguese Assembly of the Republic, peace protestors released hundreds of white doves in the ornate and historic chamber in an effort to illustrate that they wanted peace. Reagan, not missing a beat, thanked them and said, "Thank you. We want peace as well!" He cleverly turned a disruption into an agreement and skirted a diversion from his prepared remarks. But then he had a special talent for that, unlike most of us speakers when we are put on the spot and left searching for a clever way out.

What Is the Value of a Bond with Your Audience?

What does a genuine and positive relationship with an audience produce? Why do we need to be so mindful of the audience? Do they really matter? Well, of course, without an audience, there is no speech. Without listeners, there are no talkers. Today we have sophisticated algorithmic ways of measuring audience responses to in-person speeches as well as those carried on media outlets or on social media platforms like YouTube. These responses can make or break an investment in a new product, a political nomination, the rise or fall of public company stock prices, and the public popularity of consumer products and services. Most every program or conference operator or host asks participants to rate speakers. Also, if you are represented by an agent or speakers' bureau, they will want to know how highly you were thought of by your audience in order to secure future gigs for you at the highest remuneration rate. If nothing else, that should motivate you to care about your audience.

Typically, a speaker invests a significant amount of time preparing for a talk, and may have traveled a long way to reach the speech location. There are also many motivations and purposes for a talk—to sell something, promote a new book or a product, raise money, provide scholarly analysis, inspire and motivate, share new scientific or technical discoveries, or to educate. The point is that you will have invested time and thought in your content and presentation, and you will be put under the spotlight to perform. Every speech, no matter how short or humble, is a performance and should be thought of as such. The best speakers are ones who know they are there to perform and entertain. That adds a patina or shine to the presentation.

One of my least favorite experiences as a speaker was one week after I had suffered an injury to my leg and was in a walking cast. This was a county-wide speech, and I did not want to disappoint the audience, so I canceled my airline tickets and asked my wife to drive me. She said at the podium I looked ashen and as if I were hanging on for dear life. Nevertheless I persevered with the speech. The audience was unruly and largely inattentive, something I had never experienced before. Furthermore, afterward the hosting organization refused to promptly pay my travel fees, which we had negotiated prior to my signing on for the engagement. It was not pleasant. What could I do? I was the performer and I did my best for them and then promptly left that town as quickly as possible!

What each speaker is looking for in a relationship with the audience will vary. Twice each year we host a competition called Deal Ring where we train a class of six speakers who are all investment managers. Once trained on how to make the perfect pitch, we put these managers in front of investors. The investors act as judges. They are looking for new investment strategies as well as the quality of the pitch or presentation. Each judge may decide to meet with the manager privately, and the goal for any manager is to secure as many of these meetings as possible, because a meeting may lead to an investment of money. In addition, we host a public audience to observe the competition, and at the end they vote for the best presentation.

It has been fascinating for me, as the speech coach, to watch and listen to audience responses. There are times when I can predict the winner, and other times I have no idea who the audience will select. I do know that potential investor dollars are resting on not just how well the manager presents and how brilliant the investment strategy, but how effective the audience relationship might be. In fact, at one competition in Chicago, I felt that the audience favorite was someone who was selected because he really connected with the audience. They could relate to him. He was not glib or particularly polished. He was authentic, honest, and clear. You could tell his life was shining through in a way that the audience liked. He did not necessarily have the most effective or even successful investment strategy.

If you are a press secretary or head of media or investor relations and you are briefing investors or the press, your audience might be disagreeable or exceptionally demanding and even hostile. Your ideal disposition would be not to react but to keep your mind focused on the important facts you need to deliver. This can be a supreme challenge, but if you follow this strategy, it will pay off. Journalists have a job to do, and that is to create a news story or find some conflict in order to sell their copy. Your job is to abstain from giving them more information than they need or anything that might feed a controversy.

In dealing with journalists, your job is to provide them with specific details that will help them do their job. This is where Reagan's advice to me always came in handy: "Be a well and not a fount." In other words, provide the information required or requested, but do not chatter on about numbers or results that are not specifically requested. In the name of wanting to be friendly or in an attempt to earn their collegiality, we often think that providing off-the-record comments will bring a journalist in closer as a contact. I have tried this myself and have watched others pursue this natural strategy, but it always backfires. Journalists or analysts have their jobs to do and you have yours; they are on parallel tracks to yours but not on the same one—ever.

This advice would run counter to the wisdom you might receive from the example of Mexican president Andrés Manuel López Obrador, who is called the "Communications Magician." His practice is to personally brief the media for up to ninety minutes every morning at seven a.m. His practice is to ramble on, providing some relevant information but also explaining his thoughts on many issues and answering questions not even asked by the journalists present. Their fact-checking has apparently also resulted in some everyday inconsistencies in his stories and off-the-cuff unprepared remarks. The *Wall Street Journal* reported on his approach and cited Juan Pardinas, editor of the *Daily Reforma*, as saying, "Ironically, he's using a news conference to remove the media in their role as intermediaries and take his message directly to the people."

This approach has also been utilized by both Presidents Reagan and Trump. Reagan created his own radio show to talk directly to the American people. Trump uses his Twitter account multiple times a day to speak directly to the people, bypassing media outlets. He is his own commander in chief, chief of staff, and press secretary. His is often the first tweet read by his fifty-five million followers, beating the networks or major media outlets at times, because he often learns about tragedies and international developments as fast or faster than anyone else. Journalists see this as a direct challenge to the massive media industry, and they react feverishly to counterpunch and defend what they see as their Constitutionally protected role. Given the availability of platforms on which individuals communicate personally this trend will only grow, upending even more the role of journalists.

We are more likely to see across the world many efforts to mirror this practice than we will see a return to traditional journalistic filters. The corner has been turned, at least for politicians and their audiences. With digital platforms ubiquitously available and the preferred means of communication for an increasing number of leaders and speakers, there is no reason we will not see more direct communication between any chief executive and his constituency. This also applies to other

Obama was the first US president to use Twitter while in office and was credited as an intelligent speaker.

private sector leaders, many of whom already use these platforms to communicate.

For corporate news, it is likely we will continue to release
data through respected media channels that report on business and the economy as well as social issues of concern. But
ultimately this phenomenon will disrupt and change as well,
largely because of security issues. Traditional media—the way
people are informed via television and print reporting—is
nearing the end of its cycle, which has had a seventy-year run
for TV and hundreds of years for print journalism.

Personal devices and individually curated media platforms
will be the next channel for communication of all types. But
how will they be policed and held accountable for honesty and
integrity? The users of social media will be in control of how
and when they receive news and entertainment. The question
for public speakers and their audiences is how this migration
will affect the practice of delivering in-person, live messages
of value. I would guess these developments will make personal
talks even more important as a counterpoint, if nothing else,
to a completely electronic universe. Personally delivered information and analysis may become more valued and essential
but will surely be delivered on more diverse and new platforms
directly to the user of this content.

How Do You Deliver Bad News to an Audience?

We have been taking about audiences and how to connect with
them and effectively deliver messages that they will find credible and listenable at the same time. But what if your message

to an audience is not positive, upbeat, or inspirational? What if you are imparting information that is challenging in nature or reporting to investors that you are shutting down an investment fund and that their money will be returned—or not? How do you report poor quarterly earnings or project a series of losses? At our investment manager competitions, I have seen new managers with no money at all under management and poor investment performance who still have the humility and courage to seek dollars from sophisticated investors and stand and deliver to an intimidating crowd. I am not sure how they do it.

What if you are a local chief of police in a small town that suffers a tragic loss of life in a terrifying shooting incident and you are called in the middle of the night to report on global news platforms? What if you are a school principal called upon to assess a shooting at your school or an outbreak of some contagious disease. I am always fascinated and watch with awe at how well these community representatives do in speaking before an audience of millions and broadcast around the globe and endlessly replayed and analyzed with all the legal constraints and straitjackets they must honor in not mentioning certain names and alleged circumstances. To me it's a miracle more of these extraordinary communciators don't break down in many of these situations.

Generally, leaders of all types and at all levels receive almost no training on how to handle a crisis in communication or even everyday stock losses, a lapse of ethics, or a personal tragedy of some type. Training in finance or marketing appears critical for business leadership—and it surely is. To me, however, the ability to effectively communicate to customers, shareholders, and the public at large should be the absolute first qualification—especially in media-aggressive times, with disruption in almost every industry, and new ways of conducting and assessing business and office protocol and professional behavior.

Consider recent ineffective media presentations by mature, highly educated, and experienced corporate leaders such as Boeing CEO Dennis Muilenburg, speaking in the aftermath of the two 737 MAX disasters in which 346 lives were lost. Or consider General Electric CEO Larry Culp's MSNBC interview and discussion of the significant challenges of keeping GE alive and growing—after which GE stock took a tumble. Or Chip Wilson, CEO of Lululemon, saying that his clothes were not appropriate for fat women. And keep in mind Elon Musk's gaffe that sent Tesla's share price in a downward spiral.

You might wonder where and how these leaders prepared themselves to speak to the public.

In spite of their lack of training or coaching, these individuals are basically good people who seem to show a lack of common sense and above all any effective basic communicator training. All these serious gaffes were perpetrated in large media markets with significant audience numbers—not to mention the aftermarket for these mistakes among industry analysts, investors, talk show hosts, and academics at business schools writing cases about poor industry decision-making. These poor performances will not quickly be forgotten. Future audiences will hear about them for years.

One of Nancy Reagan's rules was always to put out bad news on Friday night and good news on Monday morning— that is, if you have the ability to do that and the timing works. And she wasn't kidding. If you put out bad news on Friday night, it might have a shorter life span with little attention from your audience. On Monday you want your good news to sail through and be repeated again and again during the whole week. However, with dominant 24/7 social media platforms overtaking traditional channels for news, Nancy Reagan's rule is not as pertinent today—but you get the gist. You can be sure we took her rule seriously for our work on the president's Theme for the Day Team, when we designated each day of the week to pursue and spotlight specific topics and policy objectives, also mindful that the early days in any week might be more productive for media coverage and attention during weekends and holidays being much slower.

As for the ideal and most productive times to post on various social media sites, you can now determine that by industry, by day, down to the minute. For example, health care companies might have their best results on Instagram at nine a.m. Eastern time on Mondays. In general, all social media posts are best received and read between nine a.m. and four p.m. Monday through Friday, and from one to nine p.m. on Saturdays. There is general consensus that the best time to post on LinkedIn is from ten to eleven a.m. Tuesday through Thursday because that is when recruiters and business people focus their attention on the site.

Sunday is the slowest response day for audiences on all social media platforms. While these are broad parameters, there are plenty of increasingly sophisticated and shifting algorithms available to assist you in meeting your target and pulling from your audience the optimal response rate.

Into the life of most speakers and leaders will come the necessity of communicating to an audience bad results or news or even deaths and tragedy. This responsibility is never convenient and often excruciating, or at least it should feel that way, and yet it is part of the job. Your audience will be waiting to judge you more harshly during a time of stress because they may be suffering themselves, or even be the victims of the bad news you must share.

Here is how audiences want to hear you share an unwelcome incident:

1. **Show how genuinely sorry** and personally moved you are to have to communicate this news. Get yourself out of the way, but somehow show how distraught you are over this (without a show of anything fake). Make your remarks out in the field—that is near the location where the tragedy or bad news might have taken place or inside the plant or factory with your team around you in solidarity. Men should elect something softer than a suit and tie to wear; women should select something modest and not too sophisticated. If you are an official in uniform, by all means wear it and appear in a neutral setting that does not detract from your detailed message.

2. **Connect with the affected people.** If you as a spokesperson do not readily see how this news will affect people at various levels, then by all means consult with someone in the company who will get you up to speed. Sometimes excessive compensation packages and too much money can be an insulator from understanding how the common worker might see things. Flying around in private or corporate aircraft with personal security guards might immunize

upper management to how vulnerable the regular hourly or salaried worker feels and might react.

3. **Express gratitude** for everyone's support, express thanks to people, possibly law enforcement or first responders, who have been tireless and helpful. Talk about your dedication and work to resolve and improve the situation and your resolve and commitment to do better on behalf of the company or your team in the future.

4. **Offer to keep everyone in the loop** with updates and open communication and offer a designated and secure hotline for calls or texting if necessary, for which you should volunteer when you can, to talk with people directly and hear their feelings about the issue.

5. **Promise to get to the bottom of the problem** and express your regret that this has affected good people. Your job is to win them over but never through self-justification or self-righteousness, just as we have been talking about with any audience. The way you do that is to express your sincere sadness, as if these things had happened to your very own family. Do not be defensive. If you have built up a reservoir of trust and respect among your employees, the community, and the media, your sincerity will be accepted and recognized as real and authentic. If you are showing your audience a new face and attitude, you might need some time to convince people of your sincerity, now that this event has occurred.

6. Have a plan or strategy in place, including how you will talk and communicate about these things. Do not let this tragedy or loss come up unexpectedly without advance training and preparation. You have plans to remediate cyber security breaches. Now you need to have a plan to remediate personal communication failures. Focus on your audience and who will be in it and what their concerns and position will be in any untoward and unexpected losses. Role play with your colleagues and take it seriously. There can be a lot at stake.

In addition to the excellence displayed by first responders who report directly to the community and the media as calmly and candidly as possible to relate horrific details from shootings and other calamities, I salute Walmart. It is an example of a company that is utilizing the plan I have suggested. Their corporate leadership has learned from their mistakes in the past and in the last two years they have done a superb job of quickly assessing collateral damage, supporting their employees, customers, and community members, and in moving the story along positive and short-lived lines.

How to Talk about Yourself to Your Audience

One of the seven deadly sins of public speaking and one of the easiest and most surefire ways to raise the fourth wall of separation and segregate yourself from your audience is to refer to yourself in the first person and to take credit for everything you have accomplished, invested in, studied, operated, owned, or observed in your life. Even though this seems an obvious pitfall we see rampant examples of it everywhere.

Have you ever received a holiday card or letter from a family that has three children who each founded a tech company, just made their annual trip around the world in a private jet, and had a building named for them at Harvard—and they want to tell you all about it in their annual report to their select and exclusive audience? When the phenomenon of family holiday missives started, we read them with interest, a lot of amusement, and a little jealousy. And yet, curiously, those out-of-touch brag letters still circulate. It seems the urge to celebrate yourself is greater than the self-awareness that your audience does not want to hear all the details about your good fortune over the past twelve months. What may be acceptable is a little bit of family news tacked on to a holiday greeting minus the details of the leather seating in the new boat and the home theater you installed. Your good fortune should remain with you and your family.

The same is true for self-obsessed people who stand and deliver messages to live, taped, or televised audiences. Recently we attended an awards ceremony where there were four speakers at a rather formal dinner that included a program of impressive music and an opera singer. What really spoiled the lovely feel of the event, however, was the first speaker. While you would imagine that an award ceremony focuses on the individual who is being celebrated, our first presenter focused on himself. He was especially talented at saying nice things about his famous friend but always placed himself at the scene he was describing—as an indispensable enabler and contributor to the featured man's life.

If the man had graduated from an Ivy League school, then his friend followed him in cap and gown. If the honoree started a company, the presenter was the man who funded it. On and on it went. I was squirming in my seat. My wife and I couldn't wait for the gentleman to conclude and be seated with the other guests. Thankfully, the next speaker offered a complete contrast of self-contrition and modesty, taking care to not once refer to himself but rather to focus completely on the friend he was honoring.

We have all heard and endured endless puffery from speakers. The marvel to me is that it appears these proud people seem desperate to impress their audience and to seek approval from them, when in fact the opposite happens in the minds of the very audience from which they seek affirmation. In reality, it just does not work. We have all had bosses who blew smoke at their employees about how great they are—and yet we never believed them.

I had a boss once who was so obsessed with his intelligence that he made his staff endure lectures that were really meant to control us and to impress us with his sheer brilliance. In truth he didn't convince us he was anything but pathetic. I have always wondered if the people who speak to impress are actually frightfully insecure on the inside, as our parents told us growing up, or if they actually feel they are superior human beings to the rest of us. More and more in the land of extreme sports, and extreme accomplishments and wealth, I have begun to think it is the latter. Whatever it is, it does not bode well for a speaker who desires to please the audience.

We have also had to endure political speeches about how

smart and sensitive and honorable and worthy candidates are. In our hearts we know they are just like us and should simply act and talk that way. In a certain respect, that is why we have pancake breakfasts and barbeques with political candidates. Voters want to see up close if the people they might vote for are like them. This is a good metaphor to consider when it comes to our own orations. Our audiences may need to know something about our background or achievements to lend authority to what we are saying, but they are also examining us closely to see if we are someone like they are. There is one little rule that can save a self-focused pitch. Rule out the use of the words "I" or "me." Find other ways to communicate. You will find yourself in a better and more productive relationship with your audience if you do this.

When Talking about Yourself Works

There are times when it is impossible not to make a reference to something we have accomplished or action we have taken that supports the content of our message. In fact, it may even be central to our message and interesting to our audience. If used sparingly, the record and experiences of our own lives can be interesting and essential to making talking points more meaningful and illustrative. This requires a clever turn of posture where we are really looking at ourselves and our own life just as our audience is as we talk about ourselves. It is a sort of credible, honest, impersonal way of talking about ourselves that doesn't result in the audience pinning the arrogance label on us and shutting us down as a result.

Here's one example. At one time I was informed I was to receive an award from a nonprofit organization. I was honored to be selected but wondered how I should shape my acceptance remarks. The organization helped with an ingenious way for me to accept the award. Instead of asking me to make lengthy remarks at the actual ceremony, they sent a film crew to record my thoughts on a video they produced about me. I was the only person with a speaking role in the video, and I was interviewed by an off-camera producer. She proceeded to ask me a series of questions that allowed me to share how much this institution had meant to me and how critical I thought it was to my various accomplishments.

If you follow my reasoning here, I was able to focus the main spotlight on the institution giving me the award while I was also able to retell my own story, giving a lot of credit for any accomplishments to this organization. As the principal actor in the film, I was talking about myself for sure, but I was focusing the credit away from me, onto the impersonal institutional partner that had prepared me for my life's accomplishments. I think the film achieved its objective of honoring the organization and me. That was a nice solution. Not all are that easy.

Another example. At one time, as a board member, I created an annual award to be given on behalf of a major art museum to leading art collectors. The first award was given to David Rockefeller, with whom I was acquainted, and for whom I held the highest regard. Mr. Rockefeller was a worldly man of outsize accomplishment, while remaining the consummate gentleman who always made time for friends and warm personal relationships, despite his responsibility for running a major bank and a family fortune, among many other cultural and philanthropic organizations. I introduced Mr. Rockefeller on behalf of the museum and then asked the chairman of the board to bestow the medal on him. I stood near him as he made his acceptance remarks. There was no need to either congratulate himself nor act with faux humility. He talked with extraordinary grace and gratitude about the opportunity he had to develop the eye and ability to collect art together with Peggy, his beloved wife. The audience was rapt.

He was a person of obvious renown, telling his extraordinary story, giving insights, providing personal anecdotes about rare places and rare instances in exotic places all over the world. I know the audience was transported right with him as he described just a little of his life as a major collector and donor of art to many highly regarded museums. What an example of a person at the pinnacle of accomplishment, and yet quietly bonding with his audience merely because of the shared love of art. This is where personal stories engender respect and ego dares not to whisper.

As public speakers, we want to emulate this type of person. No, we may not have the monumental personal respectability earned through generations of dedication to public service and the gentleness of a man over ninety years old and mellowed by age, but we can still learn from his example how to talk about our lives, if and when we need to in our own talks, with gratitude and awe.

CHAPTER SEVEN

Own the Room with Storytelling

More Than Anything Else, People Want to Hear Stories

We heard a talk not long ago delivered by a woman who had survived a concentration camp and had, by her own wits and exceptional intelligence, escaped and had gone on to excel as a physicist and to also discover several important pharmacological solutions. It was important for us to know the details of her remarkable life and her triumph over horrific adversity to illustrate what a life dedicated to scientific inquiry could mean for those in the audience. She described how her life almost didn't happen.

To make the story memorable, she added dramatic vignettes describing the suffering of her family. We felt like we were on a lifetime road trip with her as she vividly relived her life story for us. If you asked me today, I could retell her story in detail. If you asked me to recount the other aspects of her speech, they were not as easy to recall. The point is, if you want to be remembered, tell stories. If your life has not been as dramatic as our friend the Holocaust survivor, tell someone else's story. Read biographies. They are storytelling at its best. I once told the story of how Thomas Edison would nap with his head on a pile of books so that it seemed he could absorb scientific inquiries even while asleep—and to his factory hands, it appeared to work. That was not my own story, but it fascinated the audience. I had learned it in a well-written Edison biography. If you don't have your own story, tell your friend's story or a friend of a friend's story. It all works.

I grew up reading a feature in the *Reader's Digest* that came reliably every month to our mailbox. It was called "The Most Unforgettable Character I Ever Met." I would grab hold of the issue as soon as it arrived and would not let go. It was the magazine's most popular feature for all the years it ran. No wonder. It was colorful narration. I guess we love stories, because even if they are not about us, they really are. Humanity, as different as we all are, is lumped into one basket of similarity. I know that this *Reader's Digest* series helped me build a moral for my own life and made me feel I wanted a life of service, reading about these heroic, simple people. I still have some of these features saved in my file of most valued writings.

Let's find out what storytelling is all about, anyway. It has been with us since the beginning of time and is the main reason we know anything about the beginning of time. Stories were the principal way history was kept and passed from one generation to another. There were no books or YouTube. People gathered around in tribes, families, and communities and told stories about their ancestors and about recent events.

Stories were the way news was conveyed. Life itself is a story waiting to be retold by someone. Oral histories continue to fill a unique role and are now a part of museums and libraries, including the National Archives, where there is an effort to capture life's stories as they may tell critical facts missing from the current written or recorded narrative.

This is all going on despite a trend in contemporary life to dismiss history, because for some it may seem politically inconvenient and because of diminished academic requirements for it. Because I have an unusual last name, I was curious to find its source and derivation. That has plunged me into genealogy to attempt to learn more about its origin. This is not really a story of interest to others outside my own family, and yet it fascinates me that its origin is French and that at some time and in some way my progenitors were probably rose garden tenders who were given the name de Rosier, later translated into Rosebush, to mark their profession!

I think of the stories of life retold in book form and in speeches by the extraordinarily gifted Lynne Olson, who has uncovered previously untold stories about World War II and shared them in ways that are captivating and surprisingly true and yet mostly never heard before. How could this be? There have been hundreds of books written about that war, and yet there is still new material and more stories to tell—really, stories that must be told. Lynne Olson spins these stories in her books, like *Citizens of London*, *Last Hope Island*, and *Madame Fourcade's Secret War*, in ways that make you want to read all day long and call in sick to the office so you don't have to leave Olson's highly descriptive writing. She talks that way as well. I have heard her. She pulls you into the story, and for a time you virtually go and live in London during the Blitz with bombs raining all around you, or fight with the Resistance in France.

At one time I was the interim head of a coed military boarding high school. Some of the students came from homes of strife and suffering. What these students overcame by adopting a lifestyle of discipline and leadership was where life stories were really made. Some students were setting the stage for their own lives as they lived there, and many have become highly successful in life. These are students who have plenty to tell in speeches because many of them can reflect on life's colorful triumphs and tragedies and it is more and more acceptable today to do so.

Pixar, which is a company totally dependent and built on story spinning and telling, has a director, Pete Docter, who defines storytelling this way:

What you're trying to do, when you tell a story, is to write about an event in your life that made you feel some particular way. And what you're trying to do, when you tell a story, is to get the audience to have that same feeling.

Everywhere around us are stories: in film, biographies, fiction writing, and in painting. Storytelling is used in addiction rehab and other therapies because it involves an understanding and awareness of the human condition. There is a natural structure, rhythm, and cadence in storytelling done the right way. The stories of heroes and underdogs can be related in speeches, and people especially love those. Authors like

Stephen King have built publishing careers on their ability to tell a gripping, frightening story. Stories can be deeply emotional and personal, or cool and graphic, but for speeches they must be purposeful. That is the difference. A speaker uses stories to make a point.

A good example of this would be our friend and the retired curator of Northern Baroque Painting at the National Gallery of Art, Arthur Wheelock. Arthur is a sought-after public speaker and professor precisely because he delivers the factual through the dramatic. He tells the history of the Netherlands and the origins of Dutch painting through the lens of the economy, social order, and much more, through the personal lives of not only the artists of the time but the people with whom these painters associated. His job had been to purchase and curate a noted and highly valuable collection, but the way he tells its history and adds to its luster is through storytelling. After all, every painting is a story being told either in exact depiction or idealized through the dramatic eye, imaginative mind, and creative brushstroke of the painter.

In addition to storytelling through art, film, video, music, and dance, stories can be told for more mundane but useful purposes—like customer satisfaction for products or for travel. Today the best type of instruction on how to build or repair equipment is through video-recorded directions from a person actually assembling the piece. If you want to know how to repair virtually anything, you look on YouTube for the story of someone else who has successfully completed a repair, and they will show you how to do it through their own story and practical demonstration. Because video production is now in the hands of anyone who owns a phone, stories, some of them works of fiction, are rapidly proliferating and are broadcast on multiple platforms, like Instagram. But despite this growing phenomenon, your job is to fit a story to your thesis and key points and to drive value through storytelling to the audience. How, in specific terms, can that be accomplished?

There are many speeches being given today that are entirely based on overcoming personal adversity, some of it graphic and disturbing. What the Holocaust survivor gave her audience, however, was more than emotion. She provided us with a road map for our own lives, a template, a way forward out of darkness into light, out of poverty to success. That is what people want to hear. They do not want to remain in a state of feeling emotionally sorry for the speaker and awed by her tribulation, with all its gory details. They want to know how to get out of adversity and turn it into spiritual or material profit of some kind themselves.

The overabundant marketplace for stories that just focus on personal abuse and endurance, however, may now be somewhat waning, perhaps because audiences have become saturated with an unbroken record of sadness. No one has to walk farther than over to their phones and open up to read all about it. Stories of crime, abuse, and personal degradation and woe are ubiquitous throughout the day and night. Some of it true, some of it fabricated for various reasons. The whole human condition is exposed to anyone who will read it until, ultimately, they become desensitized and immune to it. They have heard of every kind of terror and abuse, many times over. We have had a generation of that.

We are now moving on to report impact—in every sector. We are now beginning to measure and report on everything we do by its impact—including giving and attending speeches. So it's logical we want the stories we hear to show impact. Impact on the environment, on our education and learning, impact on our community, our houses, our jobs, our well-being. People are less interested in hearing depressing and dramatic stories without solutions. This is where speeches of the self-help and motivational type are migrating: to impact. Is it any surprise? The audience wants to know the return on investment for their even being present and listening—perhaps for even paying money and traveling a distance for the privilege. The audience is asking accountability from the speaker and increasingly some sort of validation.

Oprah Winfrey pioneered and introduced much of what we have today as acceptable dramatic storytelling about our own lives of adversity and survival. Even some highly successful and well-meaning tell-a-tale pastors participate in these sessions. And then there is the mightily successful and influential Brené Brown, a speaker, best-selling author, and coach who has, thousands of times, recounted her insights, struggles, and issues. She is incredibly successful in bonding with her audiences, men and women, because she makes them laugh and cry. She makes fun of herself and includes stories about how ignorant she was about choices she made earlier in her life. She relates how she struggles and prevails—and still does every day. Sounds like all of us, right?

She is also fearless when it comes to presenting her story and her solutions, but always points these tales in the direction of how they apply to her audience. She is a one-woman industry and shows no signs of stopping or failing from some kind of controversy. Most important, however, her key to success is that she is not promising to make change happen for you; she is demanding that you stand up and make the change for yourself, to rewrite your story. There is a difference. She may be selling you salvation or at least a better life, but she is not denying you the profit from having to save yourself and find your own discipline and productive relationships along the way. The audiences drink that in and then have something to do for themselves. They can see impact reflected in their own lives from listening to her storytelling and reading her best-selling books and listening to her podcasts.

That is how she became a best-seller and has remained that way for each of her books. This is not passive oration. It is full of personal conviction with outcomes and impact. Of course, you say, that is because of the topics she selects, and that is true to a large extent. But what Brené Brown does and the way she does it could be applied to a speech about invest-ment strategies and the roots and struggles of democracy as well! She would still make it to the top. It's about how she does it and the connection she has with her very loyal audience.

The entire sector of self-help and personal motivation speaking has grown to become a massive industry from which some of the most successful public speakers are drawn, icons like Louise Hay, Stephen Covey, and Wayne Dyer who held public broadcasting audiences at rapt attention for decades. Since it became more acceptable to talk about yourself on stage in the late 1980s, sometimes describing in excruciat-ing detail your struggles with addictions, and abuse, and even near-death experiences, not to mention romance and relationships—talking about yourself became an entirely new wave and way of speaking. Social media platforms blew it up even more becoming the major sponsors of an exaggerated and massive trend.

Speeches alongside books, webinars, YouTube videos, podcasts, and other web-based productions account for a flourishing $5 billion annual industry called self-help. According to John LaRosa of Marketdata, LLC, there are more than 5,000 motivational speakers in the US earning more than $1 billion per year, with the top ten of all these speakers earning a combined total of $200 million annually. But this industry, which was a product of the baby-boom generation and heavily subsidized by them, is fading. Some podium speeches have been replaced by personal coaching done over Zoom, Skype, webinars, or in-person consultations. The entire personal coaching industry might be thought of by some as questionable, but no mistaking it, there are millions of personal coaches advertising their services around the globe. As for their drawing a personal audience to a destination to listen to their speeches, that is becoming a more competitive prospect.

Making Storytelling a Part of Your Everyday Life

We began this section talking about the long-respected precept of never or rarely using the personal pronoun "I" in your speeches and never or rarely talking about yourself. And yet we have just had a robust discussion about the sub-sector of the public speaking industry focused on personal storytelling and self-help. The personal storytelling in the self-help and motivation sector is done for the purpose of capturing the interest of the audience in a way that they can relate to. The content becomes the narrative of your personal suffering or triumph, and once the audience becomes hooked on that story, with all its attendant details, they can, ideally, follow the speaker on a solution track, where the speaker may even be endorsing or selling a product or coaching to go along with it. Don't leave the story hanging there. Apply it to a moral or an economic solution or impact and help guide the listener through it.

Let's say you tell a true story of your own life's challenges and that you are midstream in solving these problems. That's okay. Share that feature with the audience too. They can relate. You do not have to be perfect to be relatable. In fact, the opposite is probably most true. One exception, however, is not to leave them mid-sentence, so to speak. You might say, "And of these challenges, I would tell you, I have still not found the perfect and final solution...but I would tell you this...I have learned that if anything will get me to home plate it would be..."

The other use of personal storytelling we have highlighted is where the impressive life of one survivor might become a brave retelling of historic proportion that inspires the audience to use this material for their own gain and as a role model or for filling in gaps in historical knowledge. It is interesting to hear the story of famous figures or even people telling and retelling the stories of their own families if they reflect on history or other topics of intrinsic value to the audience. As always, remaining faithful to the interest of the audience is key.

Every speaker should be a market researcher determining the key topics your audience would like to hear about. Do not go too far afield of what people want to hear. For example, as a person who has always been interested in reading obituaries of interesting people, especially the long and detailed ones published in the *Times* of London, I have felt that speeches could be developed based on the historical accounts contained in these colorful retellings, and these could make up a small industry of talks based on this, always-churning, content. These obits make great storytelling fodder for speeches and talks.

When our daughters were little and we took road trips in the car, we often listened to audio books. One series was a sort of general-audiences-approved spy thriller about Mrs. Emily Pollifax, a white-haired woman in her sixties who signs up with the CIA to be a spy. A dozen books featuring this protagonist were written by Dorothy Gilman between 1966 and 2000. These highly descriptive formats led the four of us on mystery tours all over the world as we listened to every detail on driving trips between Washington, DC, and New York. The storytelling was compelling and the reading professional grade, and we were admittedly a captive yet very appreciate audience, all the way to the end of every book and every adventure. We have never forgotten the storytelling of Emily Pollifax in our family.

When I was in the production studio recording my own audio book *True Reagan*, I had a moving and somewhat emotional experience related to audience development and bonding. The recording work was tough and took five days, eight hours a day. The producer was outstanding and worked with me to bring meaning to the words people would only be hearing over audio. One of the most significant things he shared with me about expressing the content I had written and my voice tone was to speak as if I loved my subject. That stuck with me. To speak as if I loved my subject. Well, that was easy, because my subject was Ronald Reagan, and my admiration, respect, and love for him came easily. And yet here this brilliant young producer was telling me to think deeply, as I read, about how much I appreciated our fortieth president.

We worked day in and day out, including many redubs and re-recordings because of my gaffes or because the super-sensitive mics picked up my hungry stomach growling. After all this editing, we were finally at the end of the book, and as I recorded the last sentence of the book and put down the text in the recording booth, I heard, through the earphones I was wearing, someone crying. And it was a serious cry, not whimper. Slowly I realized that it must be the producer. I waited a brief second and then asked, through the mic, "Are you okay?" Now by this time we had become friends, but I was unsure if I had done something to offend him or make him sad or emotional. His answer surprised me.

All along he had unselfishly coached me, telling me to love my subject and my audience, and he seemed to hold nothing back. Now I was hearing him through tears say this to me: "You see, all these years I was taught to hate Ronald Reagan, and you [meaning what I had written about Reagan] made me love him." This was startling to me because he had never prejudiced or compromised our recording session together by discussing his previous misconception of or prejudice against the president. His genuine restraint and his change of heart were something I will never forget. This experience taught me that love is conveyed through the thought of the speaker to the audience, and that made all the difference. The production booth where he sat was not particularly near the sound studio where I was reading and recording. The producer was not looking at me as a live audience would look at the speaker. And yet the message was conveyed in a speaking voice in a way that moved the audience that day in the recording studio. It was an unforgettable lesson.

The Ultimate Connection with Your Audience

While there are many ways to connect with your audience, and we have discussed quite a few, there is one that surpasses all other strategies. To love your audience, to be happy about being there in the room or hall with them, physically or virtually, to appreciate the distance they came for your talk, to appreciate them for just being there and listening—that is the ultimate bonding force. This can also be achieved in a recorded or broadcast speech.

When I worked at the White House, I had innumerable opportunities to hear great speeches and to watch performances by many notable people and to become acquainted with quite a few of them. I spent time with the venerable stage and film actress Mary Martin—the originator of the role of Peter Pan on stage and film. As we were standing talking on the expansive South Lawn of the White House one afternoon, I asked her why she was such a success with her audiences. She responded right away, wrapping her arms around me in a big hug and said, "Why, Jim, it just worked for me because I was born loving people. I have always loved my audiences, and they gave the love back to me. That is where the bonding happens!" That was all I needed to hear and to remember. That is the most important message and the best advice I can share with you as speakers.

CHAPTER EIGHT

The Perfect Trifecta: Audience, Content, Delivery

Accelerated Delivery Is Like Speed Dating

Most audiences look to speakers for educational or business content, intellectual stimulation, topical controversies, self-help, or they are looking simply for entertainment and diversion from the ordinary in everyday life. Most audiences are drawn to speakers whom they expect to be above average in their knowledge about a particular topic or topics and in their ability to communicate and they expect they are surely smarter than the other guests attending, watching, or listening in. These are the expectations.

To make an exceptional presentation you need to have a perfect blend of original and well-thought-out content paired with superior delivery. These two elements, combined and blended, support each other. We have all heard highly educated speakers present learned and interesting topics, but who project poorly in their delivery. As a result, they do not rate highly. College professors can do that. We have also heard speakers who are glib and fascinating speakers, but in the end, we are left with emptiness in the content category. This is the beauty of working to combine both forces symphonically. Expectations run high for a speaker who can effectively blend content and delivery. This is why the level of perceived risk for the speaker also runs high, and that sometimes stimulates and triggers fear and insecurity in the speaker.

Writing speeches or considering what material to offer and how to package it to fit the attention span of an audience often distracted by the magnetic powers of their cell phones is difficult for even the most compelling speaker. Twenty-two minutes used to be the accepted standard maximum amount of time the speaker could reasonably expect to hold the attention of an audience. Thirty minutes has been the standard format of the network and cable television shows including advertising before, it was believed, the watcher would turn the channel.

This timing is now being recalibrated, and ten-minute show segments are being tested alongside multiple story line development in most dramatic and even news shows today. That makes it tough for speakers, who can typically only handle one story line at a time and usually take more than ten minutes to deliver a worthwhile speech, especially if they are being paid a significant fee for doing it.

The longest speech I have ever delivered ran seventy-five minutes, and I thought I was running the risk of the hook— being pulled off the stage because of the sheer boredom and tedium of the audience. And that was an after-dinner speech at a university where I was the only speaker, and perhaps people had been served a sufficient amount of alcohol and were relaxed enough not to mind the lateness of the hour. The lighting in the convention center was also ideal with the audience in low light to make everyone feel attractive and entertained, and the presenters well lighted so they could be clearly seen and in focus.

I would never have talked so long if I had felt the audience was squeamish or bored. I felt we were in a groove, and they seemed to be wanting more from me on the topic. The audience attended and paid for their tickets that evening because they were most of them dedicated to my content—the topic at hand—and I was mostly telling stories related specifically to it. For that reason, I felt it was acceptable to continue on, risking perhaps not being invited back. I would never advise anyone to continue speaking more than a max of forty-five minutes, and here I was thirty minutes in violation of that rule.

It turned out to be the longest talk I have given from a dais, and it was recorded and broadcast for classes at the college and to the public as well. Aware of the lateness of the hour and the length of my talk, I was more than surprised, after talking so long, to receive a standing ovation—perhaps they were standing in relief that I was ending! I doubt I would ever talk that long again, with some rare possible exceptions.

Perhaps, as I mentioned, delivering an after-dinner talk helped, but with high caution I would strongly suggest you not continue talking if you happen to be the last speaker *before* lunch or dinner, when people are ready for food and drink. That is called the "death watch" time slot for speakers. Always try to avoid that, if at all possible. You might get trampled upon in the rush to the doors on the way to lunch, and you may not have the line of people from the audience who want to talk with you afterward or perhaps engage with you professionally.

There is much more time pressure for luncheon speeches than at a dinner talk. At midday people may have to get back to work. If you are scheduled to speak at lunch during a conference, it may also be the time that people step out to make calls or meet up with contacts in the hall, or if the meeting is in an urban area, people may go out for a walk. It is also awkward to have people eating their lunch during a program. I typically suggest people eat the main course and the speaker begin when dessert is being served. Don't overlook that, as the main attraction, you may want to take responsibility and direct this process; help the audience feel comfortable continuing to eat their meal and suggest that the servers continue their work during your talk.

I have spoken at hundreds of conferences where the manager, owner, or organizer never really informs the audience whether they should be eating or not during a talk. You should take the initiative and help make people feel comfortable. It's a part of bringing down the fourth wall and being a Sherpa, host, and guide.

I have also spoken at conferences where, during breakout sessions, a horde of people walked out of the room where I was just being introduced to hear someone potentially more valuable or to make calls or meet contacts. There is something unnerving about this. Don't take it personally. It is a part of every conference. By all means, do not comment on it or draw attention to it in any way, as I have heard some neophytes do. If you have an audience of ten or ten thousand, you may find one person whose life is changed by your content and delivery. Do not be distracted or threatened by numbers, whatever they might be. One productive connection or relationship that may come out of a speech, if you desire that, could change everything.

If you are the president of the United States, you can make speeches that illustrate the blend of content and delivery, where the audience is typically compelled to remain until you are finished—perhaps even for security purposes. You can talk as long as you need to, within the time constraints of televised coverage, up until you might lose your audience to a televised football game or other sporting event.

Trump's 2019 State of the Union speech ran as the third longest in history with 5,250 words spoken over eighty-two minutes. His talk length was surpassed by President Bill Clinton twice, who gave the longest and the second longest State of the Union speeches at eighty-nine minutes (9,190 words) in 2000 and eighty-four minutes for the one in 1995.

George W. Bush's speeches averaged over fifty minutes, and Obama's averaged just over one hour. The length of these speeches is largely dictated by the breadth of material to cover and the addition of heroes to be introduced—which began with Reagan. Trump in 2019 had an unusually large number of guests to introduce. Nevertheless, the trend is longer, which runs counter to the demand for shorter speeches by most speakers who do not have the privilege of living and working at 1600 Pennsylvania Avenue.

Given the pressure to shorten speeches and compress more value and impact into briefer presentations, speakers are also talking faster in order to hold the listener's attention and push out as much information or entertainment value as possible in a limited, more compact amount of time. It remains to be seen how the shorter time and faster talking phenomenon affect the

President Clinton was a big talker but he was also very smart and could deliver a lengthy speech without notes because he mastered his subject.

profession of public speaking and the ability to communicate essential information—especially in political circles.

The first time I noticed the trend of faster talking through content in prime time, as we discussed in chapter three, was on the *ABC Evening News* with David Muir—who early on won the ratings wars in part due to his "rapid delivery." He reads the teleprompter fast, and when you watch him and listen, your mind races right along with him. The high-energy tempo is more in line with the way we hear many voices today and is in sync with the fact that the human mind can process words faster than the average human voice can speak them.

According to Ray Hull, a professor of communications at Wichita State University in Kansas, the average person speaks at a clip "equal to 145 words per minute," but now due to the need to say more in the compressed period of time allowed by more audiences, the "rate of speech has escalated to an average of 160–180 words per minute." As a result, it seems logical that speaking in a rapid tone will increase the urgency, attention, and excitement of the audience. You can test this for yourself by typing 180 words on a sheet of paper or your screen and then reading them, marking the time it takes you. Speaking fast also makes the speaker seem smarter. No wonder David Muir and ABC won the race among prime-time news broadcasters for a younger audience and higher ratings.

Snapchat and TikTok provide communicators with fifteen seconds to convey an image, a dance, a song, or a speech—before it disappears. With that type of experience becoming more common, the speeches of the future will surely become more compact and abbreviated. The bar of tolerance being set by the audience to convey content is being time-compressed.

At the Deal Ring competition, we train our investment managers to make their pitch in only five minutes, and if you cannot stick within that limit, plus allowing fifteen minutes for questions and answers following your pitch, then you have not gotten the investment model across to your potential investors. The time clock is always running fast, but sharp judges who are asset allocators know how to pick winners quickly.

Not all groups can assess complex investment strategies as quickly as our judges, and it is possible that young children and other groups need words of instruction spoken more deliberately and slowly, as do those not hearing the spoken word in their native language. Adults in their prime process words at a faster clip. Senior citizens may also require a slower pace due to cognitive issues or hearing loss. As a speaker, you should take all of this into account when you face your audience—or risk perplexed looks on the faces of your listeners. Take stock of the age group, and if you are speaking to seniors, be especially sensitive to the pitch and volume of your voice, because there could be many people in any audience with hearing issues.

All Public Speaking Is Selling

President Trump is a master at keeping his pace and energy level high at his rallies, and he talks at a high volume—mostly in the shouting range. It's not that his words move particularly fast, like David Muir's, but his energy level is sustained, and his voice, though not particularly pleasing, is compelling because of his volume and the way he punches his lines and repeats them—even to the point that when he uses a teleprompter he will restate words for emphasis that do not even appear in the text, rather than selecting new ones. He also has a slight New York accent, which makes his sound a little different and broadly recognizable in a crowd. He veers off the written speech copy and ad libs frequently and not particularly eloquently or in a focused way, but this keeps the audience on full alert. The audience waits for this. It keeps them at attention.

He is the master salesman, always keeping the audience engaged in one thing or another. There is nothing slow or tired about this presentation. His energy level is at the normative level of a man in his twenties or thirties. There is no slowing down. The audience can anticipate this, and it makes them feel engaged and excited. This is how he keeps his audience entertained and focused on him and on his message. He also adds elements of surprise. You never know exactly what will come out of his mouth, and you have the feeling he doesn't either, so you keep waiting for it—even focused on it. This is how he holds his audience.

At his July 2019 Orlando, Florida, campaign launch for a second term, he brought his audience up especially close when he asked them their preference for his 2020 slogan. He had them vote by show of hands. They were so fired up for both slogans, it was hard to tell which choice won. This speech was laced with references to what he was doing for them, the crowd, the people. The audience felt that in their hearts. Watching Trump in action is like a certain type of speech lesson—not all perfect but full of useful examples. In some ways his manner of speaking is reflective of and perfect for a disruptive era because he created much of it. These are useful lessons, though, because the disruptive era will continue long after Trump leaves office.

His messages are delivered something like the way a carnival barker would who must sell tickets to a side show because he is making a commission based on how many tickets he sells. In this way he motivates his audience to take action—to figuratively buy tickets for the show and be entertained. This approach comes out of his background as a salesman, so it is natural for him. For Trump, as well as for many, perhaps even most speakers, all public talking is selling.

While much, but not all, of public speaking is about selling, my own motto is: *"Always sell without selling, convince without convincing, impress without trying."*

If someone has an opportunity to take control of the mic and sees the opportunity to promote a specific product or service or even to sell themselves, the fourth wall of resistance may go right up. There is a knee-jerk reaction by the audience to protect themselves from being sold and the big red mental stop sign goes up. The assertive seller sometimes creates the opposite of the desired effect. Some in the audience may physically or mentally walk out, especially if they feel they were invited to attend under false pretense. I have often led panels where, despite the participants being told that they cannot mention their products or attempt to sell, they do it anyway. They cannot help themselves, or they may feel so under pressure by their sales organizations to do so that they leap over these rules and surge ahead. I have had this happen many times. It grates on the other panelists who do abide by the direction of the producers. Those who are disobedient lose their audience as a result, because they are not fooling anyone. They are going in directly for the sale.

One exception to this is at industry conferences like CES—the Consumer Electronics Show in Las Vegas—which annually attracts nearly 200,000 people. At CES attendees expect to hear from industry CEOs and others about the details and future promises of new technology. This is hard, creative, and well-targeted selling—the best in the world. The annual auto shows also follow this practice, as do some other industry conferences, especially where there are tangible products to look at, touch, and feel. The difference is that the audience attends with the expectation that the talks will be sales pitches.

An additional exception are the plentiful online and televised home shopping networks where people tune in to be sold items. There are sometimes talks or interviews with celebrities on these sites as well. It is all focused on one thing: sales!

Here are some suggestions about how to sell content without the hard sell.

1. **Invite an unbiased, well-qualified guest speaker** of some renown to lecture on your industry broadly and have them address issues they might deal with in their own sphere of influence without mentioning your products at all. An example might be inviting a guest to speak about the degradation of drinking water from lead when you represent a filtration or purification company; or having the head of a governmental agency speak about clean water—not to endorse your product but to be present alongside of or to introduce the talk.

2. **Invite your chief economist to talk** about the impact of international trade on the investment market without ever talking about your branded investment products. I once invited the head of the Federal Reserve Board to dinner to talk about the history of the Fed. He never once mentioned commercial banks or bank policy, although there were bankers present as guests who might have gained some potential clients in the crowd. It was an enthralling talk and made for a memorable evening.

3. If you are the chief marketing officer, then you might make the main feature of your talk **the trends in your industry** generally, without making any sort of ask related to your specific products.

4. If you really want to talk about your company or are invited to do so, then **tell personal stories** about how you got involved in this business. An example of this might be in the clothing or fashion business, where brands are built on designers talking about their approach to their concepts. More recently, car companies are having executives talk about design as well, without offering discounts on specific models.

5. At every event, **ask your introducer to announce your title, position, credentials**, and explain what you do. Then you will not have to justify or sell yourself, because everyone will know what you do. One word of caution is always to work with your introducer and review the copy

prior to going on stage. This is critical, because you cannot always assume that an introducer knows the best way to describe you. The ideal would be to have the introducer practice their remarks in front of you prior to going on stage.

One practical example: I launched a social impact investment fund. I have spoken on many stages about this growing trend but never asked anyone to invest. I always discussed the rise in capital allocation to impact strategies, how the millennial generation ushered this phenomenon in, and how I got my start in this field in my very first position in wealth management and philanthropy. My design for these speeches was to build confidence in me by sharing my background in the strategy, thereby encouraging potential interest in the fund during the discussions following the talk. Everything today is measured in terms of impact, but audiences do not always want to know they are being hit up, especially by a fundraiser or salesman.

The Symmetry of Successful Content

With all the competition for and traffic jams in words and accelerated delivery in increasingly brief sounds-bites or perorations, how do you make certain your message is heard and thoughtfully considered in a way that brings about results? It begins with crafting a message worth hearing—ideas that can gain and retain a high berth in the minds of the listeners. Increasingly, what most speakers are attempting to achieve is to mobilize their listeners to take some sort of action, which might be to invest in the speaker's business, purchase a product, stand up to an injustice, support a philanthropic cause, or to plainly help themselves flourish. Audiences are used to this motive but typically want the message delivered in a nonconfrontational and somewhat oblique yet captivating way. For the most part, audiences do not respond well to a hard-nosed or direct sales approach.

In some ways, every speech could be viewed like a homily or sermon in a church. Every week the preacher has a responsibility to craft a message that inspires the congregation. To help accomplish that, the minister first has to know the needs of the congregants—the issues that are uppermost in the minds and hearts of the parishioners—just as a public speaker does for their secular audience. It might be global, community, or personal issues—there are plenty to select from, such as an opioid addiction overtaking the town, teenage gangs, depression, unemployment, or fear and lack of self-affirmation. Next, the preacher needs to address these issues in the content portion of the service during his personal message.

The message or content, the delivery, and the audience must fit together like a perfect trifecta, to be memorable and impactful. Otherwise the minister has lost not only the attention of his parishioners and guests, but he has lost a significant opportunity to help and heal, stimulate, move, and inspire.

I have always called President Reagan an evangelist. He was an evangelist for freedom. Almost every speech was like a sermon with all the best elements. More often than not when listening to his speeches, I thought I might have been sitting in a church pew rather than in the staff seats near the podium. Reagan had thought in college of pursuing a preaching career. Instead he became a secular preacher and imagined a lot of his world audience figuratively sitting in the pews in front of him. Reagan knew the structure and cadence of the ideal sermon and instructed his speechwriters to follow it. Reagan, who was a politician giving sermons, employed this basic seven-point format often used by the most successful preachers.

Here is a preacher's approach to creating and delivering a sermon which any speaker may successfully follow.

1. Reveal and announce the theme or the topic in the first paragraph and relate it immediately and directly to the needs of the audience.

2. Explain how this topic came to mind or why it is important to focus on.

3. Relate it to some great writing or thinking on the subject.

4. Tell up to three stories that illustrate and drive home the point of the talk.

5. Return to and repeat the focus and objective.

6. Call on the audience to take action or to put this topic and solution to use in their own lives or for the greater good.

7. Conclude with an inspirational quote or statement—which is the preacher's way to seal the message and give the audience an uplifting send-off.

Here is an example of Reagan the preacher before a mournful nation the evening of the *Challenger* shuttle explosion in which all seven astronauts, including the first schoolteacher in space, Christa McAuliffe, perished. Note how Reagan follows the format above in a speech judged by many to be one of the finest in history.

Ladies and gentlemen, I'd planned to speak to you tonight to report on the state of the Union, but the events of earlier today have led me to change those plans. Today is a day for mourning and remembering.

Nancy and I are pained to the core by the tragedy of the shuttle Challenger. *We know we share this pain with all of the people of our country. This is truly a national loss.*

Nineteen years ago, almost to the day, we lost three astronauts in a terrible accident on the ground. But we've never lost an astronaut in flight; we've never had a tragedy like this. And perhaps we've forgotten the courage it took for the crew of the shuttle; but they, the Challenger *Seven, were aware of the dangers, but overcame them and did their jobs brilliantly. We mourn seven heroes: Michael Smith, Dick Scobee, Judith Resnik, Ronald McNair, Ellison Onizuka, Gregory Jarvis, and Christa McAuliffe. We mourn their loss as a nation together.*

For the families of the seven, we cannot bear, as you do, the full impact of this tragedy. But we feel the loss, and we're thinking about you so very much. Your loved ones were daring and brave, and they had that special grace, that special spirit that says, "Give me a challenge and I'll meet it with joy." They had a hunger to explore the universe and discover its truths. They wished to serve, and they did. They served all of us.

We've grown used to wonders in this century. It's hard to dazzle us. But for twenty-five years the United States space program has been doing just that. We've grown used to the idea of space, and perhaps we forget that we've only just begun. We're still pioneers. They, the members of the Challenger crew, were pioneers.

And I want to say something to the schoolchildren of America who were watching the live coverage of the shuttle's takeoff. I know it is hard to understand, but sometimes painful things like this happen. It's all part of the process of exploration and discovery. It's all part of taking a chance and expanding man's horizons. The future doesn't belong to the fainthearted; it belongs to the brave. The Challenger crew was pulling us into the future, and we'll continue to follow them.

I've always had great faith in and respect for our space program, and what happened today does nothing to diminish it. We don't hide our space program. We don't keep secrets and cover things up. We do it all up front and in public. That's the way freedom is, and we wouldn't change it for a minute.

We'll continue our quest in space. There will be more shuttle flights and more shuttle crews and, yes, more volunteers, more civilians, more teachers in space. Nothing ends here; our hopes and our journeys continue.

I want to add that I wish I could talk to every man and woman who works for NASA or who worked on this mission and tell them: "Your dedication and professionalism have moved and impressed us for decades. And we know of your anguish. We share it."

There's a coincidence today. On this day 390 years ago, the great explorer Sir Francis Drake died aboard ship off the coast of Panama. In his lifetime the great frontiers were the oceans, and an historian later said, "He lived by the sea, died on it, and was buried in it." Well, today we can say of the Challenger *crew: Their dedication was, like Drake's, complete.*

The crew of the space shuttle Challenger *honored us by the manner in which they lived their lives. We will never forget them, nor the last time we saw them, this morning, as they prepared for their journey and waved goodbye and "slipped the surly bonds of earth" to "touch the face of God."*

Getting to Work: Drafting Your Content

There are five essential foundational elements in the development of any successful content, speech, presentation, or message.

1. Become acquainted with your audience; learn what they want to hear.

2. Define the principle takeaway, your gift to the audience.

3. Develop a compelling, useful, message on a subject on which you are an expert.

4. Create a rationale and strong defense for your message.

5. Maintain the ability to control the message through to the end of your speech.

Let's discuss these in order.

1. Your Audience Is Your Fuel

There are two forces at play in every speech. Some speakers miss this point completely and instead just focus exclusively on their speech and their own speechwriting—leaving out the audience as an essential part of the preparation. In fact, there is no speech without an audience of some kind. Your topic should come from the inspiration you gain from thinking and learning about your audience. This is the absolute best way to invent your topic. There is no better advice I can offer than this.

An example might be as follows. You have been a foreign service officer serving in China. You learn that your audience is concerned about the future of China and its strategy for global expansion. That becomes the subject of your speech. Another example might stem from your expertise as an architect, and you will deliver a talk about modernism as a trend. You research your audience, only to learn that the audience may be interested in modernism but that in their city there are strict building codes that limit architectural styles and materials and only small lots are available for building. You would therefore address your specific remarks to those concerns as they relate to modernism.

A third example might be a talk you have been asked to give on the future of social media and its utility and entertainment value. You learn that the majority of your audience will be young parents. Researching a bit more with your host organization, you might learn that these parents are terrified about social media use by their young children. You would add great value if you choose not to ignore but address these concerns to the extent you are knowledgeable about them and help them know how to handle social media issues with their children. Even if you are handed your topic or you are giving a specific book talk on a fixed topic, you can still lean in to the audience by curating your remarks to meet what you discover or even surmise that they would be interested in.

And what about a title for your talk? If you have not been provided a title by your host or program organizer, then craft one with some pizzazz, a little mystery, and allure. Bring them in either by your own excellent renown and credentials or by the topic. However you design it, your title should clearly represent your content in a way that will draw people in, especially if there is a timely hint of controversy or even scandal about your topic. Most speakers are inexpert about titles. Ask your family and friends about it, and they will help you, as outsiders, with what will stimulate and sell. The title should be crisp, memorable, and repeatable by the audience when their friends and colleagues ask them to cite the title of the talk they heard yesterday. The title should state honestly what you will offer in your talk, not circumvent it or make an attempt to be too clever or to make the audience work too hard to figure out the focus and value.

We are defining audience in the broadest sense. They may be participants in a webcast, watching a video, reading an email blast, or part of a live group from one to one million watching and listening to a presentation of some kind. Since most speakers want something to happen (impact, enlightenment, education) in the minds of their listeners as a result of their talk, it is of primary importance to determine the makeup of your audience and just how they might be affected by your content and over what type of platform they are hearing and processing it.

No batter ever hit a home run without focusing intently on the ball as well as where he wants it to go. That means first understanding the personality and skill of the pitcher, the mental and physical topography of the field, and the weather in the area. No golf pro addresses the tee without knowing exactly where the cup is positioned on the green. That means first researching the density of the green, its rise and fall, how it will respond to the speed of the ball and what will happen to the ball once it lands there. No quarterback reaches the wide receiver without a play plan and the skill to send the ball through the air and meet its target. Speakers should identify themselves as athletes, where conditioning, research, and preparation are not only essential, but can make or break your success.

Physically seeing your audience—if you are present with them—doesn't mean you necessarily know who they are or why they are in the audience. Eye contact is no substitute for really knowing who you are looking at. It is no substitute for due diligence about the audience and what they might want from you. After all, this is a transaction between you and the audience. It is dynamic and not passive. I have seen out-of-touch CEOs or team leaders even look at their employees and expect them to be respectful when the leader has little knowledge about them and shows little genuine interest in them or their lives.

I have also been on speaking tours where I am addressing multiple audiences each day. How, you ask, would I be able to have a sufficient degree of knowledge about all of those audiences? You gather facts as you roll. Ask strategic questions of your hosts, Google news about the local community. It's not hard once you commit to it and accept that it is a part of your required due diligence on the road. Similarly, if you are giving a presentation to employees, shareholders, investors, don't go in blind. Become acquainted a bit with their concerns, issues, and mood. They will appreciate your doing this, and your communication ability on a two-way street will be perceptibly improved and you will be rewarded.

At one stop, which I will never forget, I was about to address a crowd at a magnificent historic North Carolina resort nestled at the base of Grandfather Mountain. I had been briefed, in general terms, about the audience, which was made up largely of residents of this impressive summer resort colony. Just as I was about to step up to the podium, a distinguished gentleman approached me and asked me to add to my talk an analysis of Tolstoy's published writing about Abraham Lincoln. He thrust a copy of the writing into my hand with the decided expectation that I would honor his request.

This was not a part of my prepared remarks, but I was curious about the boldness of the last-minute demand as well as its fascinating content. I told the guest I would do my best to accommodate his request and quickly read the remarkable piece published by Tolstoy observing the one hundredth anniversary of Lincoln's birth. In it he bestows the highest praise on the fourteenth president of the United States and calls his character one for all nations to exalt. My view of and interest in the audience immediately deepened when I knew someone like my new friend would be attentively listening. As a result of scanning this piece, I altered some of my own remarks to make them more reflective and provide a deeper analysis for this learned crowd.

Sometimes the speaker has to exercise spontaneity to make a revision on the spot, as I was required to do that evening. In a way you could say the guest was testing me. But I took it as an alert to consider making subtle changes to improve my content and to include what he asked for. If you can find ways to especially please your audience, you have drawn them up closer and won their admiration—even for attempting to address a concern or special interest.

Spontaneity and authority can make good partners for public speaking. Mastering your content enough to be able to add last-minute unscripted remarks that enhance your message may significantly improve the whole experience for everyone. Again, as opposed to a dry and rote speaking experience, you are looking for something positive to happen during your presentation in the way of new inspiration in your mind or in the minds of the audience.

On another speaking tour, I found it comical that although my announced topic was President Reagan, more often than not the crowd, including even many men in the audience, wanted to discuss the more controversial and mostly misunderstood Nancy Reagan. I found myself very often veering away, simply by demand from the audience, from my primary topic, to make them happy by telling personal stories that revealed more of the character of the famous and somewhat mysterious first lady. The audience may make demands on you as a speaker, and it is always better to attempt to fulfill what they want if possible. This does not mean you compromise your material or point of view to satisfy one or two attendees. You have to weigh and discover the right balance.

Any effective speaker needs to learn a few things about the audience and spend a little time researching their interests before beginning the preparation of the content. You might ask if there are any sensitivities you should be aware of. These would be things that might have happened in the community where you are talking or in the organization you are addressing. This doesn't mean you will necessarily mention these things in your talk, because it is often good to stay away from tough topics that are personal to their organization or community. Taking the time to ask these questions, however, shows your regard for the people you will address and will help you deliver a more meaningful speech.

You need to ask yourself, with humility, why the audience might be motivated to listen to your message. Are they schoolchildren, adults, the military, sophisticated financiers, moms, prisoners? Might they be suffering, seeking hope, strivers, highly educated, students? Your audience might even be your very own team members or colleagues. Do you know enough about them to match your content to them?

There are research and audience assessment firms that have the ability to provide you with profiles and descriptions of virtually any group or demographic, and this guidance will help you in preparation of your content and help you target it for the result you are seeking. They will tell you if your viewers are young, old, highly educated or not, predisposed to your message or opposed. You can also research previous talks on your topic that were successes or failures with a listening audience, and this will help you adhere to what has been said before or lead you to deviate from it.

When Pope John Paul II traveled to his native Poland in June 1979, two years after he was elected head of the Catholic church, the world—and especially the controlling communist party in Poland and elsewhere—was taken by complete surprise and alarmed at the size of his audiences in all the cities and villages where he went. It is estimated that he spoke and offered a mass to more than five million people during his nine-day trip to Poland.

Given the extreme opposition of the Kremlin and the Polish communist party, the pontiff had to strategically plan his messages and the content of his masses to illustrate his desire to honor his faith and that of the general population who still considered themselves Catholic. At the same time, however, he was keenly aware that he had not only a world watching, but communist monitors as well. After all, this was a man who had been an actor in his younger years and was keenly aware of an audience. Many of these speeches were carried live or reported on extensively throughout the world.

One person who heard the voice of Poland's native son was Ronald Reagan, the future president of the United States, who

Pope John Paul II had to deliver masses to the Polish people that would inspire but also not threaten his communist adversaries on his heroic first trip back to his homeland after becoming the head of the church.

sat thousands of miles away in rapt attention. With a tear in his eye, he said to an adviser, "Now, this is a leader I can work with."

In his superb book *A Pope and a President*, Paul Kengor describes the powerful effect the pope's trip to Poland had on Reagan, who was in the "audience" virtually and observed the pontiff's trip to his homeland on television, and then decided to appeal to his own audience about the pope's visit and about Poland itself. According to Kengor, "And speak out Reagan did. He went into the radio studio and recorded several nationally syndicated broadcasts on the Pope's trip and on Poland's history of communist persecution." Following up on what the pope said to his audiences, Reagan reached out to American audiences with his own speeches on what the pope accomplished in his nine days in Poland. He included these remarks in this passage from one of his radio addresses at the time:

> *For forty years the Polish people have lived under first the Nazis and then the Soviets. For forty years they have been ringed by tanks and guns. The voices behind those tanks and guns have told them there is no God. Now with the eyes of all the world on them they have looked past those menacing weapons and listened to the voice of one man who has told them there is a God and it is their inalienable right to freely worship that God. Will the Kremlin ever be the same again? Will any of us for that matter?*

Just as the pope understood his audiences in Poland and wrote his homilies for them, so did Reagan, far away in America, write his radio speeches with his audiences in mind. You see the interplay between the speaker, the content, and the audience here with both men.

President Trump is also keenly aware of who is audience is, and he curates his content to feed directly to what his audiences want to hear from him. He is always looking for a reaction. Any reaction. He thrives on this. But if you analyze the Trump approach, the content he offers his supporters is dramatically different, especially at his rallies, than at a State of the Union speech. At the latter occasion his content will be more measured and designed to address prominent or key issues in ways that are not uniformly agreeable to his entire audience but will appeal to many. That doesn't mean he is unaware that what he says may be antagonistic to some. It is just that he has different content for different audiences. This is unusual for politician whose words are always recorded and over-analyzed, where consistency over disruption is typically prized. His approach does reveal, however, that his messages are designed for specific audience response.

To prepare for and design content for your audience, start by identifying:

- Material and subjects they might respond well to;
- Prejudices or special circumstances they may bring with them;
- Information or data they might respond to;
- Subjects to steer away from;
- Outcomes they might be seeking; and
- Age group, economic, and educational level they represent.

2. Articulate the Principal Takeaway

The definition of a "takeaway" is a key fact or idea to be remembered. This will be the focal point of your presentation. It is the useful product, offspring, or result of someone hearing your presentation. It is the "so what." I always like to ask that question. What is the "so what" when thinking about the strategy for any policy, invention, pitch, or the start-up companies often found in tech incubators around the world? You may be creating something, and here we are talking about speeches, but it is good to ask in all these situations about the "so what." The answer provides you with the justification for moving forward, a proof of concept, where you deliver the goods and have impact.

Very often I attend presentations given by start-up company founders. It is inspiring to hear about new solutions and opportunities. The talks, pitches, or speeches given around these start-ups and the process of explaining them to investors are always interesting to me—especially when so much is at stake for these entrepreneurs. The takeaway is securing funding, plain and simple. Only a small percentage of these start-ups will survive funding rounds, but the ones that prove their value and communicate it effectively typically win. I have noticed that many of the start-up originators frame their presentations around a personal story.

These are stories that illustrate a human reason for creating a business solution in the first place. It might be an air filtration company built because their mom suffered from allergies. Or a better solution for baby diapers started by a mom of six children. The stories give validation and make you want to listen and surely to fund them if the business plan makes financial sense. This is built into and is one of the best features of a free-market system, constantly churning and providing space, runway, and funding for new inventions and solutions of all kinds for a waiting marketplace. The personal stories that form the core of their presentations really make it work for me. It makes you see why storytelling is the best route for any speech, whether or not it is a pitch for a new company.

The one presentation and pitch I remember most vividly was given by a young inventor who created an instantly deployable tourniquet for use on the battlefield. He explained how many deaths in battle are caused by excessive bleeding and that there had been no good solution for this. He had seen this problem during his own military service and described it in full and excruciating detail. His new invention was adopted for trial use by the Pentagon, and his firm is now marching forward with production. The "so what" was amply proved by a combination of the technology, answering an urgent call from the marketplace for a better solution, and by the financial and marketing ability of the founders and their advisers.

As you begin to sketch the outline for your talk, imagine the finished product: the speech completed, delivered, and the audience leaving the hall or exiting the webinar. Ask yourself what they are saying about your talk. Did they grasp your main points? Did they apply these to their own lives and special situations? Did they track or follow your outline? If your topic is focused on a humanitarian crisis, are they more committed to engagement of some sort? If you are an entertainment speaker, is your audience walking away with a smile on their faces, relieved of some stress or strain? Happier because of what you shared and how you shared it? If your topic is physical fitness or nutrition, do you think many in your audience will begin your suggested regimen or diet?

Below are three examples of how you might begin to define a takeaway. After you read these, complete one sample sentence for yourself and you will be on your way, en route to the next step in your preparation. Keep in mind that your goal for a takeaway should be ambitious enough to make you stretch but realistic enough for you to accomplish something significant in the time you have allotted to you. Do not denigrate or limit the material you have to present. Always view it with a high level of expectation, even though your own speech might not be on the level of a State of the Union. It is still significant material to you and to your audience. The takeaway is where you set forth your expectations for yourself and your message. It is a rewarding exercise.

Here are the examples of solid and defined takeaway statements.

1. "I would like my audience to know more about the life of Dr. Martin Luther King than they have ever known before, and I would like them to be able to identify key qualities of his character they could emulate in their own lives."

2. "I would like my audience to be more aware of the dangers of lead in drinking water and as a result to be more careful about the water they drink."

3. "I would like my audience to be enlightened (or possibly scared) about the complexities of and personal

risks to them of cybercrime and the rise of identity theft and how to protect themselves against this potentially costly menace."

Now, try this on your own. "I would like my audience to know———."

Once you have your takeaway, this can become your thesis. Every speech needs a thesis or a main point, which is like the trunk of a tree that grows upward from the roots of your thinking and from which the branches of the trunk sprout and provide fruit and nourishment to the trunk. One cannot exist without the other.

3. Developing a Unique Message on Which You Are an Expert

As we've noted throughout these pages, the place to begin with the preparation for any speech is to develop a clear, coherent, and cogent message. Even if you have employed a speech-writer to do this work for you, never forget this one thing: *you own the speech you deliver, and you must take responsibility for its content and how you deliver it.* Whatever you do, do not deliver someone else's speech. By that I mean do not attempt to deliver a speech that does not honestly represent your expertise, knowledge, or experience. That would mean for example that although I would like to deliver a speech on quantum physics, it would not be accepted by the audience, because that is obviously not my field of expertise.

Your speech has to be seated in your credentials. On the

occasion that I have stretched my breadth of knowledge and had a curveball question thrown at me, I retreated in such humiliation that I pledged not to overstate my expertise or to mislead the audience again. It's a hard lesson to learn, because generally you want to appear to be an expert. There is something about standing at a podium or speaking on a video that swells the pride and threatens to lead us over the limits of authority to places where we are not prepared or knowledgeable enough to walk securely.

It was often said, usually in protest, that Reagan was just the deliverer of great words not his own, words formed into speeches by brilliant speechwriters. Not so! Reagan worked on most every speech from the start, forming its structure and agreeing on basic themes and messages. Then he would typically edit the copy several times, including even in the motorcade just before his delivery. His hands and his ideas, ideals, and values were always found throughout his speeches. He was also a speechwriter's dream, because his basic precepts never deviated, and he made them perfectly clear to the small stable of writers he kept busy at all times.

His direct engagement in the writing itself came from his experience during years on the road working as a spokesperson for General Electric, when he would write his own speeches in longhand on big yellow legal pads and hone and edit them on the long train rides he took between factory appearances because he preferred not to fly. After each speech he would change his text based on the feedback, criticism, enthusiasm, or new ideas he might have gleaned from his talks with factory workers. These notes ultimately became his political platform, informed by the people he met at the factory gate. He never deviated from these core beliefs once established during that formative period of work.

You may be given a subject on which to speak by your host or a topic by your boss—or you may have to develop your own topic. Recently I was asked by a host organization to discuss what my strategy would be for defeating the phenomenon of creeping socialism in the United States. That was a topic on which I had natural opinions but one that also required research on my part. My goal was to deliver a message that could motivate the audience to take action to help eclipse this trend and possibly to scare them a little into action to expose and stop this danger.

I decided to structure my remarks as a seven-point strategy to defeat this talk of socialism, and I aligned my points with Reagan's own strategy to help defeat Soviet-style communism. I gave the audience a structure and outline to work with so they could begin their own initiative. I observed people writing down these points and taking notes, which is always a good sign to the speaker (unless they are sending emails!) that the message is taking hold. It was well received enough that I turned it into a published article.

You might be selling a product, an investment strategy, real estate, software, plumbing products, or reporting quarterly corporate sales or announcing a political platform or strategy. You may be attempting to engender confidence in a new discovery, quash rumors, announce your candidacy for political office, or just desire to entertain. You need to know clearly why you are making this pitch and what you want the outcome to be. To have this purpose clearly in mind throughout the process is vital to its success. Returning frequently to its purpose will help you edit the speech in a way to advance your intention. It's not a bad idea to create a physical banner over your document or to post a big sticky note on your computer screen when writing it that states clearly the purpose and desired outcome of the speech.

In your speech drafts and outlines, it is wise to begin simply by stating, "I have come here this evening to share with you the details of our new acquisition so that you will have a reason to invest in our growing company." Or, "We gather here tonight to learn more about the candidacy of our fellow club member for chairman." While this may sound stiff and you may not actually begin your speech this way, you should still start your first draft this way.

Be clear about your purpose so that the audience can focus on it and will know what is coming next so that they may remain attentive and follow the development of your remarks from your opening statement until your conclusion. A useful tool might be to restate the theme or the goal up to three times during your talk to keep the audience on track. Remember, you are driving to achieve an impact or result. Once you have determined the focus of your message, then outline the speech. Your outline will look just like a template or framework for any type of superstructure with the key points and lesser points in the supporting roles. This is the most efficient and practical way to start.

I have had people say to me that they could not imagine how to begin to create such a structure for a speech. I have a simple rule to follow to fast-track your start with the speech. Sit and interview yourself as if you were a journalist. Jot down your questions that might include some like these:

- Why did you get into this business? What products do you make?
- Is there a family story behind your takeover of this firm?
- What precepts or products did you build it on?
- What was your education or preparation that helped you create it?
- Who were your role models in the industry? Did you ever meet them?
- Tell us stories about tough times and good times and what they meant to you.
- What would you have done differently?
- What would you tell anyone else who wants to build a company like yours?
- Is there any inspirational quotation you have lived by that you could share?

This is the superstructure of your speech. Just start by answering these types of questions, related of course to your own topic, and the superstructure of your talk will be on its way to polishing and editing and then the performance.

If your task is to give a product development talk, a new business or investment opportunity talk, or anything related to improving business or bringing in results, then in your preparation clearly state, to yourself, these objectives in writing. Do this as you begin your speech preparation. The more realistic and clearly stated your objective, the better chance you have of achieving your goal. Don't hide your business objective—at least don't hide it from yourself.

Here are some examples of desired outcomes from speeches you could use as templates for your own clearly stated purpose and objective:

- Sell five hundred more electric-powered vehicles this month.
- Secure fifty new requests for our new investment prospectus.
- Measurably increase public confidence in corporate earnings projections.
- Sell eight hundred new books in the next week.
- Increase the awareness of the safety issues of a new swim mask.
- Inspire more adherence to safety standards and reduce accidental deaths.
- Get out the vote or better educate voters.
- Triple the number of hits to my website.
- Make people laugh and relax.

To launch yourself in the business of public speaking, start by developing a message or speech to suit your desired outcomes even before you have an invitation or opportunity to deliver it in front of a live or broadcast audience. Having something to say places you in readiness to be invited to say it.

Let's say you have an interest in classic cars. Why not develop a talk about the value of the American-made classic cars of the mid-1950s? Another way to find a topic is to open to the editorial or op-ed pages of the *New York Times*, *Wall Street Journal*, or even your local city paper and give yourself the challenge of writing a rebuttal to something appearing on those pages. Getting into the discipline of focused thinking helps make the most focused speakers. So take your chosen topic and lay it out just as if you were applying GPS to a physical destination. Remember that your destination, in this case, is the point where you and your audience are either in agreement or in a position of mutual respectful disagreement.

Before you present to your audience, turn your propositions over in your mind, explore them with an expert, discuss them with a spouse, friend, or colleague. Go so far as to determine if your message is understandable and at least makes sense to your worst critic. Clarity of thought is essential to preciseness in your message. This is the foundation of an effective, well-received speech.

In preparing and refining a message, I have found it useful to list a series of questions and answers focused on a topic. Pretend you are questioning yourself, as someone in your audience might. The answers to these questions then form the backbone of the message that holds the speech together. If you are at an impasse in preparing your remarks, this self-questionnaire is also an effective way to break it. Let's take the subject of overfishing of the world's oceans resulting in possible food shortages as an example. This might be an outline for a message on this topic based on the questions that might come from your audience:

- How did I get the idea that there could be shortages?
- What experts do I depend upon to defend this argument? Include quotes.

- What statistics do I have that show the possible outcomes of overfishing?
- What do those in opposition to this theory have to say about it?
- What type of audience is interested in hearing my theories?
- Are there stories, personal or otherwise, I could use to illustrate my points?

Once you have the answers to these questions, you have the structure and a strong defense for your talk. If you are preparing a commencement address or an inspirational talk, your questions will be more along lines of understanding what will inform and motivate the audience. I have always wondered why there would be a need for Q&A following any talk if the presenter truly thought about what questions the audience might have beforehand and addressed them in the body of the speech.

My dad was always on the lookout for speech topics, and here is the way he approached it. For several years he was interested in how animals, especially dogs, communicated with their owners. He decided to read books and conduct research about this type of communication. His interest was based less on any fascination with our own family dog and more focused on types of nonverbal communication among animals and humans. As a result, he crafted a message about this subject, and he became a sought-after speaker on the topic simply because he found it fascinating and had developed enough knowledge about it to share it with others.

The topic had enough curiosity and mystery about it that

it gave the audience an opportunity to go home and test his theories on their own animals. It was also the kind of topic that was ideal for storytelling. There were always fascinating and dramatic stories about dogs communicating with their owners—sometimes in life-threatening situations. Today we know much more about the importance of dogs as caregivers and as emotional support animals, but his talks were at an earlier period when much less was known about the nonverbal interaction between dogs and humans. In a sense he paved the way for the dog-whisperer television show that became so popular. These talks were especially rewarding for him and of genuine interest and usefulness to his audiences.

You can follow my dad's pattern and simply begin a speaking career by finding interesting and unusual topics like he did on which you can become expert, and then begin to share these stories with others. It is even easier to develop a speaking career today than it was for my dad, because we now have multiple platforms and channels for communication and not just the limited venues that were presented to him.

Before we leave this point, let's focus on the clear and coherent description of your message. Once you have identified the focus and substance of your message or are given it as an assignment, you need to make certain you understand it and can make the topic your own. If the topic you are given does not fit with your authentic beliefs, it may be best to pass it off to another speaker. To become a vocal advocate for cement pavement on your city streets when you really believe that asphalt paving would be better would be disastrous to the outcome of your speaking career as well as to those who want to get the potholes filled! You must believe in or at least be completely comfortable with the substance of your message to be credible and to be taken seriously.

Authenticity and honesty can rarely be faked. And today there are plenty of people who make it their business to attempt to disprove what so many speakers may state as truth. Your audience may be able to tell before you open your mouth and utter your first word if what you are speaking is true. Authenticity affects the way you stand and breathe, your eye contact and focus, and is also found in the nonverbal awareness that passes between the stage and the audience, the presenter and the listener.

4. Defending Your Message

Next, you need to be able to defend your message or state a reason and rationale for it. If you propose, for example, in your speech or message, that, as we have discussed, overfishing of the oceans could severely affect food sources in coastal regions and lead to food shortages, you will need to be thoroughly educated and knowledgeable about the topic and have the statistics to back up your claims. Do not make claims you cannot personally stand behind and justify statistically. When politicians do that they often find themselves in hot water— although they don't typically mind that, because they have created controversy, and that equates with media coverage. But since the likelihood is that you are not running for president or head of state, you also need to recognize the possibly predisposed views of the audience, as they may agree or disagree with your premise or thesis.

At one of my book talks, I was approached afterward by a gentleman carrying a yellow legal pad. That should always be taken as a warning sign. I still had hope that perhaps he had made a list of all the things he liked about my talk. No such luck! He had a list, all right, one page long, of errors he found in reading my book. Whoa! That book had been edited by three knowledgeable and experienced people and had even been run through an electronic editor to catch inaccurate attributions due to other writers. And yet he still came up with these errors.

My first reaction, which I thankfully kept to myself was, "Doesn't this guy have anything else to do but find mistakes in other people's writing?" Once I quieted myself down, I gratefully accepted and he graciously offered to share his list. Would most readers or listeners have noticed these errors? Surely they were not major errors, but after considering each one and doing some careful fact-checking, sure enough, he was correct and I had been wrong. In truth I owe a lot to him, because I expect my book and transcripts from my talks to survive me and to be used for scholarship in the future, for reference purposes.

Of course, I want my text to be without defects, and he did the nitty-gritty cleanup work for me—free of charge. The changes were all made by the publisher and were reflected in the second edition of the book thanks to the brave guest at my talk who made it his business to help fact-check my book an additional time. Most any speaker will find individuals in almost any audience at the ready to judge, contradict, correct, or edit. Take them up on their reasonable offers to assist in warranted corrections, because it is better to be made aware of and correct any mistakes and to protect your reputation as a writer or speaker.

In 2002 a major controversy erupted, and for a time we observed two well-known and accomplished authors and pundits having to withdraw from public appearances and speeches because of it. Both best-selling authors Stephen Ambrose and Doris Kearns Goodwin were accused and ultimately admitted to quoting other writers without proper attribution in their own published writing. It was a major scandal in part because Goodwin served on the Pulitzer Prize selection panel and was a commentator on the *PBS Newshour.* She withdrew from both. Ambrose had so many best-selling books to his credit that he did not feel as much of a knock to his credibility and chose to ride out the controversy a bit more easily.

These scandals sent a shock wave through the publishing industry, which is akin to the speaking industry and often linked to it, and served as a warning to other speakers and writers. Now most publishers have added additional safeguards to the editing process to shield themselves against costly lawsuits that could erupt in part due to the unauthorized use of previously published materials by other authors.

We are now launching into extremely contentious and complicated territory for public speakers, far more onerous than the Goodwin and Ambrose troubles were for the written word. Spoken language, in a free society, has traditionally been governed largely by generally accepted, self-established and policed protocols or standards of conduct protected by the First Amendment. Now we are moving into a period, with no promise of receding, when discourse in some places and by some individuals is infected by toxic speech or inflammatory and defamatory remarks that are hurled at people in the effort to discredit and target. The loudest and coarsest disruptors, many of whom interrupt speeches, often make their points unchallenged, because few people have the stomach for or courage or interest in fighting back. So they "win," in a fashion.

This new way of speaking is fed, in part, by the media, who in turn sell copy and broadcast space based on controversy and language that is the sponsor of and the fuel for many a challenge to civil discourse. This language is often used strategically and can be premeditated and sponsored by organizations seeking to win public support or disrupt the support others enjoy. This phenomenon has been building for a long time with its growth sponsored by online platforms that allow communication unfettered by the constraint typically brought into play when you speak to someone in person, face-to-face. Whatever is said online can be fabricated and broadcast without accountability and largely unchecked for credibility or regard for truth, and this kind of writing has migrated and seeped into speech, speaking patterns, and common civil discourse. The credibility of what is said, although often taken as true, now calls into question Pontius Pilate's towering question: "What is truth?"

At one time I was involved in a business turnaround where I had to make decisions to help the company survive. This required us to shrink the employment base because there was not enough money to pay everyone. As a result I was the subject of a social media barrage of falsehoods attempting to discredit me. This is nothing unique to me; lots of people have had this happen to them. The shock to me, though, was when I confronted people who had written those things with the truth about the falsehoods they hurled my way, they said they didn't care whether or not they told the truth. When I heard that, it seemed to me a dark day for humanity. This is a step beyond relativism toward nihilism.

The only apparent solution to displays of toxic language is to make every attempt to be truthful, honest, informative, civil, and entertaining in our own public perorations. It also calls on each speaker to consider what is legally called "slander" for the spoken word and "libel" for the written word— both of which could be actionable in a court of law and could affect your public speaking. This includes what is called today "hate speech," which is largely protected by the First Amendment to the Constitution, with some exceptions.

To protect a free society dependent on open and honest communication, the Constitution created a wide path; nevertheless, speakers need to be fully educated on the limits of the First Amendment to protect their right to unfettered speech from litigation. This is not an area where I would profess to be an expert, but I do know that the use and selection of language is changing and is observable in speeches we all hear.

I was saddened recently when I attended a by-invitation-only meeting sponsored by a prominent business publisher, only to find that the keynote speaker felt it necessary to shout at the audience with hard invectives cursing the free-market economy and espousing something radically different, even though the organization he heads was created by the fruit of a market economy. He was surely hurling protected speech at us and was legally within his rights. It was a question to me, however, if he was within his personal rights to place his captive audience in this position. We in the audience were at the sponsor's mercy and had to remain and listen or choose to walk out.

To be useful, though, I would always recommend talking with an attorney if you are considering applying language that might enter the territory of slander, or if you are the target of slander. I have included here an excellent explanation of speech exemptions by category and compiled and shared by attorney Michelle Kaminsky, Esq., in her "Free Speech Primer" found on LegalZoom.com.

The main exceptions to free speech (Constitutional) protection include:

1. **Defamation** (includes libel and slander): discussed in greater depth below.

2. **Obscenity**: The Supreme Court test for obscenity is as follows: (a) whether the average person, applying contemporary community standards, would find that the work, taken as a whole, appeals to the prurient interest; (b) whether the work depicts or describes, in a patently offensive way, sexual conduct specifically defined by the applicable state law; and (c) whether the work, taken as a whole, lacks serious literary, artistic, political, or scientific value.

3. **Fighting words**: As defined by the Supreme Court, fighting words are "those which by their very utterance inflict injury or tend to incite an immediate breach of the peace."

4. **Causing panic**: The classic example of speech causing panic is someone yelling "Fire!" in a crowded movie theater. Speech may be suppressed where a reasonable person would know that his speech is likely to cause panic and/or harm to others.

5. Incitement to crime: Speech that spurs another to commit a crime.

6. Sedition: Speech that advocates unlawful conduct against the government or the violent overthrow of the government.

5. Maintaining Control and Command of the Message

Next, you need to have complete command of your message or topic so that you never lose control, never transfer your authority to the audience, and never play defense during your talk. Once you have your topic refined and tested and you have thoroughly defended it in your mind, then imagine you are in a courtroom hearing your testimony debated by prosecuting attorneys. You will find this preparation essential if you are a corporate spokesperson or head of investor relations. You have honed your basic message; now it is your time to defend it. Always return to your basic premise or the facts. These may be rebuffed initially by skeptics, but this is your opportunity to repeat your message and show your confidence in it. Remember, you have tested all the facts with your stand-in opponents, and you are confident in your content.

This process of practicing your defense is more acutely important today at a time when there is an overabundance of space allotted to opposing views related to almost any message. There is no reasonable excuse for not preparing yourself to be challenged on abstract theoretical and academic subjects. Your talk need not be political to raise significant questions from qualified challengers.

If you find that you or your message faces a significant challenge by those in your audience and you feel there are grounds to reexamine the content or reopen the argument, this does not mean you have lost. Keep control. Tell your audience you will reexamine your research and get back to them. Remember, stating "I do not know the answer" does not mean you are yielding control in weakness. It shows an honesty and candor that can keep you in control of your message and score points with the audience for your integrity and humility. Stating that you do not know the answer can also be an excellent tool in simply ending the debate, which might have become tedious for the rest of the audience.

At the most extreme level of message-questioning is the president of the United States, a British prime minister, or a political leader in any free and open society with a free press. Any public speaker can gain essential knowledge about public speaking by observing the way these press briefing sessions are handled. The stakes may be higher for a head of state or politician, but if your own message or platform of beliefs is worth defending, you must be prepared to stay the course and anticipate and be prepared to answer any charge against it, just as they are trained to do. The more you are able to view your message impersonally, the less personal the strife of questioning and the less emotional the interplay will seem to you.

Never take questioning of your message personally. Verbal attacks may appear aimed at you, but they are almost always about your message or platform or a position you or your team has taken that your opposition is attempting to defeat. Let your message stand or fall without you. You may be the creator, investor, writer, inventor, author, but if you can separate your creation from the creator, you will do much better communicating about it. Always use the pronoun "we" and never "I." This spreads the credit and the blame and disarms the enemy. If you take personal credit, you make yourself a rich target.

If you connect too personally with your message and make yourself instead of the message the target, you can be personally defeated. If you do assign too much personal attachment to your message, your opponents may use your personal defeat as a way to defeat the substance of your message. In certain respects, it is easier to defeat you as an individual than to defeat your message, ideas, or platform, so get yourself out of the way. If you feel your message must live or die based on you and that you have to personally go the distance to stand by your message while you mount a strong defense, make every attempt to let it stand apart from you. Let it stand on principle and the rule of law. Let it stand on the facts.

You can be sure that even in the most simple and humble speeches—to your child's soccer team, your church volunteers, your office holiday party—there will be naysayers and critics of you and what you say. There will even be people envious of your courage to stand up and talk. Your speech doesn't have to be before the United Nations Security Council or a TED talk before millions—there will always be people in the audience who will disagree or take issue with your propositions or even the veracity of your life experiences. You will notice people in the audience on their phones—lots of people. They may be texting or playing games, but they may also be fact-checking your presentation as you speak. So, make sure you fact-check first. The accepted standard for audiences now is that since people multitask using technology it is acceptable to be on your devices while sitting in an audience also listening to a talk or speech. Often now when I am speaking I look out at a sea of necks bent down and faces staring into screens. It used to be intimidating. Now I accept that it is possible to be connected technologically and with the speaker at the same time. I have traded my pique for curiosity.

While your stories may be personal, even emotional and moving, separate yourself from them. The Roman emperor Constantine had a statue erected in his honor in a prominent place. His opponents knocked the head off the sculpture. When he was told about the incident, he reached up to touch his own head and retorted, "It's very surprising, but I don't feel hurt in the least," illustrating the importance of keeping your leadership, message, and image independent from your own physical being.

You may be moved to tears by something in your speech or a story you tell, but in most cases, you should suppress the tears. It might seem at the time like an effective way to connect with your audience, but in the long run it will appear that you lost control and are weak. I have had this occur myself when on the podium, and I usually stop and ask the audience to bear with me one moment. They usually think I have lost my place or that I am searching to add a new idea. You want to feel a personal connection with your audience but not always emotionally. The audience might feel you have approached them too personally or violated their space.

Influencers are paid a lot of money to expose and promote what they wear and where they wear it, what they drive, and where they drive. But this can also backfire and can promote a lack of genuine interest through overexposure and result in a type of dangerous immunity, especially to stories of personal suffering. Revealing too much personal information, too often, can ultimately cause people to lose interest rather than to sustain it. This is where the written word and the spoken word diverge. It seems there is an insatiable drive to read and learn more and more minute details of another person's life. This is all attested to on Facebook, but remember, once another person learns everything about you or, better said, what you want them to know about you, you have lost a certain degree of mystery. Some degree of mystery makes you more interesting as a character and more likely to be heard and sought after.

I remember telling Nancy Reagan, after learning that Jackie Kennedy, still rated the most popular first lady in American history, never conducted a single press interview while she was in the White House or after, that she should try the mystery approach to popularity as well. Jackie Kennedy was vastly popular because you really knew nothing about her and because she remained in control of her image. She told you what she wanted you to know about her, which was nothing. I would say that even in a popularity contest with the Kardashians, about whom many people know everything, Jackie Kennedy would still win. All you knew about her is what the media interpreted for you. Nothing came directly from her.

President Reagan was particularly adept at this. In the days of large gatherings of journalists in the East Room of the White House for large-scale, prime-time press conferences, presidents, including Reagan, were aggressively put to a severe, unforgiving test. In the absence of these larger media events today, the political tests go on hourly, and President Trump manages these, largely as his own interpreter, responding to and sparring with his opponents or anyone whom he finds as a convenient target. Reagan left most of this hourly sparring to his press secretaries and staff, some of whom would conveniently and sometimes usefully leak news stories or become sources of back-channel information.

For the large, stage-managed press events in the East Room, Reagan would prepare for hours in what was called the family theater located on the ground floor near the East Wing garden, where first-run or old movies were shown for the first families and their guests. Reagan would be thoroughly briefed and then be mercilessly challenged by mock journalists, portrayed by White House staff. This type of preparation is still essential for any speaker who might be questioned by the media in particular or for a speaker who subjects himself to a question and answer session.

Committing to this level of preparation is the best defense against most any type of threat against your presentation and your commitment to honesty and integrity—the qualities that always win in the end.

CHAPTER NINE

The Architecture of a Great Speech

Great Speeches Come from Great Thinking

Here is something I want you to remember. Great speeches can be powerful and accomplish remarkably positive things when developed and delivered by authentic people endowed with moral character. Great speeches can equate with great leadership. It is a curious thing, though, that today, despite a surge in the number of centers focused on leadership training, coaching, and development throughout the country, we do not exhibit greater leadership skills nor do we have an abundance of inspired orators in any sector of our nation. Perhaps that is also why great speeches are rare. We need more of them, and we need to provide opportunities for their presentation. If you examine what are called the greatest speeches of all time, you will see that most were given in relation to going to war or leading a nation in some crisis. We should have speeches of all types in all fields, and they should be heralded and included in schools as the shared thoughts of mankind.

In the past, great speeches have launched armies as well as multilateral peace-seeking organizations. They have set forth values that inspired people to disrupt tyranny and slavery; they have sparked a moon launch as well as mourned a shuttle disaster; they have launched legislation and impeached a president. Never underestimate the influence for good you can unleash through this medium. Public speaking presents at the same time an awesome opportunity and a grave responsibility. Although in history this responsibility has been misused for tyrannical purposes with catastrophic results, the opportunity and need for purposeful public speaking linked to visionary and responsible leadership remains tantamount.

The courageous and learned abolitionist, and friend of President Lincoln, Frederick Douglass illustrated the inherent link between great thoughts, great oration, and great leadership in his 1861 speech entitled "Life in Pictures" when he said,

---

We live in deeds, not years, in thoughts, not breaths, in feelings, not fingers on a dial. We should count time in heartthrobs; he most lives, who thinks the most, feels the noblest, acts the best.

But, you ask, am I a woman or man with the skills needed to craft and deliver a truly extraordinary speech? Great speeches, you say, are given by statesmen, military leaders, preachers, university presidents, poets, occasionally politicians, inventors, and individuals who have suffered and worked to end suffering. We would all agree that there is no shortage of problems to be solved and issues to be addressed. Then let us also agree that a great speech could set in motion the solution to one of these challenges or provide some light or a novel approach to a fresh problem. A great speech doesn't have to be long, but it does have to move the audience and have a lasting legacy. It requires bigger than normal thinking about an issue. Great speeches are about putting thought into action. Great speeches are an impetus for action. They could also be the inspired talk you give to your son or daughter at bedtime or the counseling you do for inmates at the detention center where you volunteer.

If you feel this is a challenge you are not equipped to undertake because in general you feel that problems are too vast and complicated to assess and hard to understand, remember what X Prize founder and author of the book *Abundance* Peter Diamandis asserts in this passage:

When looking at the most pressing issue humanity will face in the next 100 years, I do not believe it will stem from those typically highlighted by the media: a scarcity of water, energy, or other resources. As described in my book Abundance, *I believe in the next 30 years we truly are heading to a world of abundance where we will be able to meet the basic needs of every man, woman and child.*

Through advances in exponentially growing technologies such as artificial intelligence, 3D printing, synthetic biology and nanotechnology, we are dematerializing and demonetizing the cost of energy, food, healthcare, and education to the point where it will be accessible to anyone on (or off) the planet at near-zero cost.

Over the next 20 to 30 years, I believe that our most pressing challenges will be driven by AI and robotics. Not in the style of the Terminator, though. Instead, my concern comes from the potential for significant technological unemployment.

What I took away from reading Peter's book is that he believes, and shows in convincing terms, that we possess all the solutions for the problems facing mankind here and now and that they are present and at our fingertips ready to be uncovered. I like that way of thinking because it makes the future bright, and the only obstacles to unprecedented growth are the limits we place upon ourselves, including on our own minds. Great speeches are spawned in unlimited thinking, dreaming, and imagination.

The X Prize, which is a cash award, was established by Peter to stimulate innovative best practices and solutions to these problems. In short, he has incentivized the rapid discovery of solutions to virtually any catastrophic or intractable problem. The X Prize Foundation got its start paying for winning solutions to oil spill cleanup and has gone on from there. The brilliance of the market economy churn is that it is based on new solutions coming into the market at all times. These new inventions require articulate speakers to announce them, fund them, take them to market. Effective public speaking is a critical asset in a free-market economy as much as in its role of safe-guarding transparent democracy.

The Ingredients of a Significant Speech

All truly great speeches, whatever their length, location, and whoever the messenger, have these four ingredients in common:

1. Vision, inspiration, passion, focus, clarity
2. New thinking or perspectives on an issue
3. Commitment to a cause
4. A call to action

Many great speeches are the product of a team of writers working on behalf of the principal speaker. Sometimes significant historical and scientific research goes into the speech drafts in order to deliver new ideas and tested theories imbued with historical documentation. If speechwriters are engaged, make certain they have the capacity to achieve your desired results. When selecting a speechwriter, make certain to review not only their previous work but study audience response to it. It might sound good to you, but what did their audiences think of it? Also see if this writer speaks your language and can write in your voice. Also review their performance from previous clients in the field of editing and the ease with which they approach making changes to suit your view of the job at hand.

Some speechwriters like to take credit for what is written and yet may not look favorably on requisite editing of their work. In the stable of extraordinary Reagan White House speechwriters, you could easily see the ones who were more interested in taking the credit and most who gave their client, the president, complete credit. Make sure you are clear about who gets the credit.

We had a revolving group of writers working on Nancy Reagan's speeches because she was very difficult to write for, and most of the president's speechwriters did not want to migrate on a permanent basis to the East Wing. Her speeches had import but, even though she was a very smart woman, she was reluctant to fully expose her thinking on many issues, and therefore her speeches were sparse, controlled, formal, and simple. When it came to speechwriting, she held back, so it was difficult for the writers to find her voice—in a way that would satisfy her. So we drifted through several long-suffering writers. Though many people assumed she sought the limelight, she always wanted to take a backseat on the public stage to the president, which most first ladies have done. I think America could take a first lady who rivals, as a speaker, her husband. I think Michelle Obama came close to that, even though she was not an elected official. In the future, we will see how the first male spouse handles speaking in public and the voice he will have.

If you are working with an internal corporate speechwriting team, you need to invest the time with these writers so that they can learn your authentic language and preferred manner of speaking. Many CEOs do not invest this time and suffer from it when there is an unexpected crunch or controversy.

Writers also need to be completely briefed on the legal ramifications of what you are able to say. These targeted remarks may need to be vetted by the media and investment relations professionals in your company. If you are the chief spokesperson for your company, organization, or even an industry, there is a tremendous weight of responsibility on what you say and how you say it. For some, our words can move markets, devalue currency, affect equity value and ultimately the job security of your employees. As a speaker, you are taking the responsibility for a lot of people you represent, even though most business or philanthropic leaders do not recognize this.

Graduation Speeches

When I think of one of the most common reasons and venues for these serious and occasionally great speeches, my mind goes straight to graduation speeches at high schools and colleges. The problem is that few people, importantly the graduating seniors, want to be there. They like the pageantry marking their accomplishment, but most are restless and eager to get on with the next stage in their lives. It is significant, though, that for many this may be the most serious speech that these graduating seniors will ever hear. As a graduation speaker myself, I can attest to the fact that this is one of the most challenging types of speech to write and deliver. It is typically short in length, has to be entertaining and inspiring, keep the attention of a usually inattentive audience, and be worthy of being reprinted in the alumni magazine for the purpose of cultivating donors!

One of the most inventive graduation addresses I know of occurred at Christian Brothers University in Memphis, Tennessee. Paul Tudor Jones, who is a graduate of the college and who is the most highly successful hedge fund manager in history, delivered the address. Never one to stand on convention, Paul nevertheless made a huge and memorable impression. After he was introduced, he asked the stage manager to bring out a large red, white, and blue bull's-eye target on a tripod and place it across the stage from the podium.

Then Paul took a bow and arrow from beneath the podium and looked at the audience, saying deadpan, "This is the only thing I want you to remember from my being here today to celebrate your graduation." And with that, being an expert hunter and marksman, he drew his bow and hit the bull's-eye precisely in the red target. Then he sat down, to rousing applause. While that might not be classified as a great speech, it was certainly a memorable one. He wanted to impress upon the graduates that intense focus on a specific target was the key to success. It was surely the way Paul worked, so it was an authentic and tested piece of advice for his audience. Paul has proved this precept for himself, and that made it valid for the graduating seniors. It could be said that Paul graphically proved the value of exquisite marksmanship in this metaphor of a speech that made his precept valid and all the more valuable for the seniors.

For a different and more conventional approach to a commencement ceremony, here are three brief excerpts from graduation ceremony speeches that show the style and earnestness of three women of accomplishment.

Condoleezza Rice, College of William and Mary, 2015

You're headed into a world where optimists are too often told to keep their ideals to themselves. Don't do it. Believe in the possibility of human progress and act to advance it. Your passion may be hard to spot, so keep an open mind and keep searching. And when you find your passion, it is yours, not what someone else thinks it should be. Don't let anyone else define your passion for you because of your gender or the color of your skin.

Arianna Huffington, Smith College, 2013

Don't buy society's definition of success. Because it's not working for anyone. It's not working for women, it's not working for men, it's not working for polar bears, it's not working for the cicadas that are apparently about to emerge and swarm us. It's only truly working for those who make pharmaceuticals for stress, diabetes, heart disease, sleeplessness, and high blood pressure.

So please don't settle for just breaking through glass ceilings in a broken corporate system or in a broken political system, where so many leaders are so disconnected from their own wisdom that we are careening from one self-inflicted crisis to another. Change much more than the M to a W at the top of the corporate flow chart. Change it by going to the root of what's wrong and redefining what we value and what we consider success.

Oprah Winfrey, Wellesley, 1997

Live your life from truth and you will survive every-thing, everything, I believe even death. You will survive everything if you can live your life from the point of view of truth. That took me a while to get, pretending to be something I wasn't, wanting to be somebody I couldn't, but understanding deep inside myself when I was will-ing to listen, that my own truth and only my own truth could set me free. Turn your wounds into wisdom. You will be wounded many times in your life. You'll make mistakes. Some people will call them failures, but I have learned that failure is really God's way of saying, "Excuse me, you're moving in the wrong direction."

So far, we have discussed the best way to create and establish a theme for your speech based on your personal or professional interests and authority. We have also talked about the perfect structure, framework, or outline—building out from the trunk of the tree that is your backbone or spine for the speech. Now I am going to give you the surefire best blueprint for a remarkable speech. It doesn't fail. It approximates what the best speechwrit-ers use. Follow it and you may be hailed as a successful speaker. It has the power to make you an inspired speaker and will enhance and increase the value of your leadership skills as well.

The Seven Essential Components in the Architecture of a Great Speech

1. Recognize and warmly thank the host and the introducer by name. Then give a bold and clear, heads-up, eyes wide-open look out at the crowd and thank them for being in the audience.

2. State the major question or challenge you will address; ask the audience to listen for and follow an enumerated number of points in your speech.

3. Tell a substantive, memorable, and multipart dramatic story that can act as a metaphor or example of what you consider to be related to the major challenge question you will address.

4. Propose a claim about the thesis, which will be your proposed remedy or answer, and defend it, as if in court.

5. Use supporting documentation or quotations from recognized thinkers, writers, statesmen, or scientists to illuminate your points and broaden the base of support in your audience.

6. Ask for audience engagement in the issue you have highlighted.

7. In your summation you have one requirement: to inspire, to send off the audience with a requirement to act on what they have heard.

Now, let's discuss each component in detail.

1. Thank your host and your audience.

Think back to the last three or four speeches you have heard. I am willing to guess the speaker did not thank either the host or the audience for attending. While I do not like to postpone or delay the launch of any substantive remarks and stories, it is critically important that you recognize the place where you are and how you got there. It was undoubtedly through an invitation, issued by an organization or a person. Sometimes the invitation is interesting itself and adds a small but vivid story to your arsenal. By recognizing them, you are giving credibility to your talk by reaffirming that someone of substance, standing, and responsibility asked you to speak. Next to that you are showing your humanity and illustrating the personal connection that is so essential to having your remarks accepted by the audience.

A simple "Thank you to Dean Smith for inviting me to talk to the senior class tonight" or "My thanks to the trustees and the director of the museum for inviting me to share a few ideas with you this evening" will work fine. Remember how we talked earlier about the fact that the audience will make up their minds about you within the first few seconds of your launch. Your humility and sincere gratitude for having been invited will add to your respectability in the eyes of the audience.

You might also mention something complimentary about the excellent work of the organization that invited you. Building up your host or host organization with recognition builds you up right alongside. These organizations may not personally endorse you or your work, but tangentially they do. Their good work rubs off on you and vice versa.

Many of the organizations that have hosted me for speeches use these events as member benefits or fundraisers. At city or country clubs all over the world one of the main events is member-attended talks. Some of these are unpaid speeches and some include a stipend. Club managers have to fill up a busy and active program of events each year, and they rely on speakers. Giving speeches at these venues is of mutual benefit. It costs you nothing and benefits you very much as a speaker if you include admiring remarks about these organizations and all the good they do for their members and their communities. I always try to conduct a little research on these organizations so that I can compliment and acknowledge them in my opening statement. This goes a long way. The same could be said for speeches at universities and colleges where I have also spoken. Recognizing and giving praise for their academic work will link you with their stature.

Next comes your recognition of the audience. Have they trudged through snow, bad traffic, had to arrive at an early hour, been brought in at the last minute by friends or business associates to hear you? Anything that shows you can relate to the audience is a plus in your favor. You might also say something like "How nice to see so many old friends here tonight" or "It's great to have an opportunity to talk with this exceptional team this afternoon." You might also recognize, if they are employees, that they have taken time out of their workday to join together at this talk and thank them for that.

If you know no one in the audience, you can still say, "It's great to be among so many new friends this evening" or

"Thanks for being such a warm and hospitable audience. I look forward to meeting many of you afterward." This is where your work begins to bring down the fourth wall of division. If you have genuine appreciation for your audience, then you will think of a way to acknowledge them with sincerity.

If there is no introducer or your introducer has done a poor job, you might need to remind the audience of your name and why you have been asked to speak. This is not a problem. You might say, "I have been invited here tonight, as the person responsible for the condition of our city streets, to share some detail with you about the new plan for paving our streets."

I have very often seen that beginner speakers, and even some with a track record, might write all of that down and even be looking at their written remarks when they speak their own name! Oh, yes, that is common. I often ask them to look up at me and speak their own name. "Okay, no problem," they say. Well, then, there is no need to look down at a written speech to remember your name or why you are qualified to be a speaker and have been invited, is there? At a minimum you should be able to utter these first few lines of welcome and introduction without a written text as you look straight out at your audience.

Another small but important point. Often when I ask people to state their name so that the audience can hear it, they mumble something incoherent or they drop their jaw and self-consciously and inarticulately breeze the name at warp speed past their listeners. Okay, so many of us have strange and complicated names. All the more reason to get it out there clearly and distinctly. Be proud of your name and state it clearly and slowly and at a volume you are certain people can hear. "Good evening. My name is <u>Austin Brands</u>." Proper names always receive emphasis when speaking, so mentally draw a mark underneath your name and remember to give yourself the same recognition you would give to <u>Arturo Toscanini</u> if you were giving a lecture on famous conductors and composers or <u>Mookie Betts</u> if you were talking about highly paid baseball players. You would not give them short shrift, so don't give yourself the short end of recognition either. It's not boasting. It is correct public speaking and helpful to the audience.

2. State the major question or challenge you will address, and ask the audience to listen for and follow an enumerated number of points in your speech.

The reason this is the only and best way to start is that you are honestly laying it all out there for your audience. Now that you have stated your intention and your focus for the balance of the speech, the audience can settle in. You will notice them doing just that—physically and mentally. They will move around a bit in their chairs, sit more comfortably, and will be thinking, "Okay, I am all in. This sounds interesting. Let's see what this person can deliver." They will move their minds to the alert signal and may start to take notes. They will pick up right away on the points of demarcation, and their minds will start outlining and hunting for the landmarks along the way.

These signals help them take notes or recall, long after you have concluded, what you said. If you leave them wondering about your thesis, and do not clearly state it, you have lost them right at the beginning and for the whole time. Their minds will follow a logical and clear path, but make sure you are on one as well! Here is where you need to be the Sherpa or guide. Don't leave your audience in the wilderness or at base camp while you are climbing up to the summit. Take them along with you!

I would have to say that based on a lifetime of listening to, perhaps, thousands of speeches, most speakers do not follow this pattern; they ramble, and it is hard to follow the outline and hints to a conclusion. Is there any outline? Sometimes I never know. It sounds like some ideas cobbled together. I have never understood why speakers proceed this way when it is so easy to follow this architecture and cash in your goodwill with the audience right from the start. If you don't know the focus of your speech, then how will your audience? It's like asking someone who has just written a doctoral thesis what it is about and they can't really tell you in a concise sentence or two. Or like someone who has just started a business and cannot coherently explain the product. I am not saying these people are insincere, not smart or well-meaning. They have just not learned how to package their communication abilities in a convincing way for an audience that might even include potential customers, students, and investors. If GPS or WAZE were attempting to map out most speeches they would show redlined traffic jams all the way to the destination. Please don't treat the audience to confusion. Help them to follow the geography of the speech. Keep them updated on where you are in your presentation. If you do this they will reward you with staying focused. This is critically important advice.

So let's discuss some specific examples of a statement or

challenge to the audience that will be the starting point of the substance of the talk. By managing it this way you are saying to your friends in the audience, "Now we are getting down to business." Here are some examples of the initial statement or challenge question and the four points to lead off. And you may ask, "Does it have to be four points exactly?" Of course not. I chose that number for illustration. I would, however, advise not going more than five (which could exhaust the audience before they settle down to listen) or fewer than three (as they might feel slighted, on the substance side). If you are a college professor giving a series of lectures, you can, of course, string your points over an entire term so you need not worry about the exact number of points. If you are seeing your audience for one hour, you better limit your points to something digestible. It's not a hard and fast rule; it is just to point you in the direction of providing your audience with an outline, and numbers do the trick nicely.

Here are five sample introductions.

"I am here tonight to share with you what I have seen on my recent tour of duty in Afghanistan and to suggest four ways I believe this conflict could be addressed more effectively."

"This afternoon I want to share with you my observations about the future of self-driving cars, and in the course of our discussion I want to share with you four ways I believe they will make our roads safer."

"Today I will be focusing on the coming expansion in the use of hydropower and the four reasons we started our own investment fund to put investor money to use in growth of this industry."

"Speaking from my past year as your representative on the school board, I want to share with you today, what I have learned and to propose four ways we can improve education in our community."

"Having been a professor and lecturer focusing on the art form of film for more than twenty years, I want to share with you my favorite examples of film at its best and share with your four ways you can look at film with a more discerning eye that may result in your enjoying and finding more pleasure in the films you watch."

These are useful examples, and I am sure you can see the logical buildup of the speech following the introductory sentence. What you are doing, in essence, is standing at base camp and saying to your team of climbers, "This is what we have accomplished so far; now, I am going to explain to you how we are going to achieve our ultimate goal of reaching the summit. I am going to save you from four critical missteps you might be tempted to make that might mean you have to abort the climb." Do you think you have the audience on board? Oh, yes. Now in this opening statement we are talking about a life-threatening situation.

Think about your opening in this way as well. You are just as much a Sherpa as that Nepalese mountaineering guide. You know your subject, through and through, and you are making an offer to enlighten, inspire, help—take the audience on a journey.

What you are sharing needs to be remembered, and offering it in this structured way will make recall easier and perhaps be put to use in a life-saving situation a year from now—you may never know. I have heard people refer to a speech they have heard years ago and also even re-state points they learned from it. If it resonates and has some sort of transformative effect on members of the audience, you have done your job well.

Here is an example of an opening statement that alerts the audience to what is coming in the balance of the speech. These are early paragraphs from one of the most noted speeches in history. The speech was given by the very learned former slave Frederick Douglass in 1860 at the Slavery Society in Glasgow, Scotland. In this brilliant speech he outlines his views on the US Constitution and he tells you plainly where he is going with it. See how he starts.

What, then, is the question? I will state it. But first let me state what is not the question. It is not whether slavery existed in the United States at the time of the adoption of the Constitution; it is not whether slaveholders took part in the framing of the Constitution; it is not whether those slaveholders, in their hearts, intended to secure certain advantages in that instrument for slavery; it is not whether the American Government has been wielded during seventy-two years in favour of the propagation and permanence of slavery; it is not whether a pro-slavery interpretation has been put upon the Constitution by the American Courts—all these points may be true or they may be false, they may be accepted or they may be rejected, without in any wise affecting the real question in debate.

The real and exact question between myself and the class of persons represented by the speech at the City Hall may be fairly stated thus:—1st, Does the United States Constitution guarantee to any class or description of people in that country the right to enslave, or hold as property, any other class or description of people in that country? 2nd, Is the dissolution of the union between the slave and free States required by fidelity to the slaves, or by the just demands of conscience? Or, in other words, is the refusal to exercise the elective franchise, and to hold office in America, the surest, wisest, and best way to abolish slavery in America?

I suggest you find the rest of his remarkable speech and read it in its entirety because, although delivered long ago, it is still timely for today.

3. Tell a multipart dramatic story that could act as a metaphor or example for your main challenge question.

The minute you have concluded your opening statement, launch rapidly into the story section. Don't linger too long in the declaration (opening section), and don't become too tedious about it. Bring on the stories, the illustrations, the sooner the better. Your audience is waiting for the stories. You start this section by literally stating, "Now let me tell you a story that will illustrate my main point." Even better, and the most triumphant way to engineer this, is to have an individual or an interconnected or multipart story to relate in each of your four (or however many) points or sections.

I can hear you now: "Where am I going to find stories to functionally and dramatically support my points? I am just an ordinary person devoid of stories in my own life!" Well, you may have more stories applicable to your topic than you think. Even the acclaimed storyteller and *New Yorker* magazine cartoonist Roz Chast admitted that she had a hyper-boring childhood and adolescence, but she turned the quirks about her family and upbringing into things worth telling and laughing about in the most uncommon common way that people can wildly relate to. In her book *The Party After You Left*, she makes stories out of the most common fears and insecurities we have about people talking about us after we leave a party and the things we missed by leaving early. It's hilarious and poignant at the same time. She captures in words and cartoons precisely how we all feel. Bingo. That is how she makes the connection to her audience.

I have heard Roz Chast speak, and her speaking voice is identical to the "voice" in her books and cartoons. She is an authentic and extraordinarily talented storyteller who would be the first person to admit that looking at her life, you would not easily find anything to wind a story around. In fact, growing up she never even left her New York City borough of Queens or the life outside her parents' apartment building, where she had one tree to look out on. Roz Chast found that writing and speaking gave a voice to her weird, neurotic, and crazy upbringing. What she found out by exposing it is that other people had lives like hers as well and could relate to her describing it. But to be a success she had to be willing to talk about it in wierd and basic terms.

But there are thousands of other memorable storytellers. Oprah Winfrey is another. She can spin a yarn about a million details in her extraordinary life of overcoming and overcoming. You tend to like to hear her stories because looking at her now and knowing something about her, the end of the story is a very good one. What she has done for others through storytelling is legendary. She is just another storyteller who supports my suggestion that you journal every day to tell yourself the story of your own life. This supports my urging you to live an interpretive life—one that you are looking at and thinking about at the same time. This is the opposite of living a mind-numbing life that may be exciting or boring but is one you don't think about and appreciate as you are doing it. People who live an interpretive life may have more stories to tell as they pick them up along life's way. I like to ride the subway in New York City. It adds color and stories to my life and enriches it. Most of my friends think I am crazy and that I am putting my life at risk by commuting to meetings this way. I find it a path to learning more of life's stories to add to my inventory.

I had a great friend, Spike Karalekas, whose life was one big story. Spike was the most entertaining person I ever knew, because he actually saw life itself as a story unfolding every day. As a speaker he could turn a boring topic into one of vivid Technicolor and excitement. He told of a dramatic day when, studying at the Naval Academy, he was out on maneuvers on the campus when he heard his name being broadcast on the loudspeaker system, and thinking he was to be reprimanded, he reluctantly but obediently answered the summons. Finally, after being tracked down, he was told to report to quarters and get fully dressed in his uniform because he had been selected to introduce President Kennedy, who was to give an address at Annapolis that day.

Sadly just a few months later he was selected to march in the president's funeral cortege in Washington, which began a years-long relationship with the Kennedy family. But as I am telling it here, it is just a list of facts or an inventory of achievements. Spike made a movie out of every story, and unlike the reaction we may have to some perpetual storytellers, Spike's stories were ones you asked him to tell and retell. You never tired of them. Part of what made them work is the pure delight he took in them. Never boastful and yet impressive, these stories are ones that he saw as amazing as his listeners did, and that kept them fresh. Spike and I used to play tennis on the White House courts. You can imagine those matches were hours long because Spike always had something he just had to tell me in between sets—usually an amazing and amusing story.

So it seems that today storytelling could become confused with talking incessantly about yourself on social media platforms. But that is not the point. That is just talking for the purpose of creating a narrative for your life, true or fabricated, and who you want your correspondents to think you are. Real storytelling is purposeful. Stories could even be told for self-effacement or to lend an example but are never useful if they are self-aggrandizing, posing, or puffery. Stories used in speeches do not even have to be about you. They might be about a friend, a child, a grandchild, a boss, or even someone you have never met but have only read or heard about.

Some people are much too reticent to talk about themselves, their lives, or the people they have met. So tell a story about a great or a bad company you have worked for, an extraordinary university you have taught at, an inspiring symphony orchestra you have heard with a masterful conductor, a football game that had a remarkable play you could use as a metaphor for your principal thesis, and what it means. Reagan himself rarely told a first-person story because he was uncomfortable talking about himself or putting himself at the center of a story.

I keep a notepad on my bedside table in case in the middle of the night I come up with an idea or a story that I want to record briefly before I go back to sleep. Printed on the top of every page is a saying written by a friend of ours, Fleur Cowles. It says simply "I Wake Up Expecting Things." That was a credo Fleur lived by. Little was ever known or discovered about her humble beginnings, but that never mattered to people who knew her. In addition to extraordinary, outsize design capabilities, for which an entire study center was created at the University of Texas, she wrote books and gave a few speeches. One of her books, titled *I Made Friends and Kept Them*, is simply an inventory of people she met and collected as friends. In spite of her other accomplishments, she felt that making friends and keeping them better reflected the story of her life. Yes, there are stories about extraordinarily famous people in the book, but there are also stories of simple and plain people Fleur met. These people gave texture to her life, and their stories became her stories. She was telling the story of her life in this book through her relationships, and it worked.

One easy example is found in delivering eulogies. I know this isn't fair because the departed often provide easy content for stories to tell in celebrating lives of friends. But look here at how the highly respected writer and speaker Jon Meacham began his remarks at the National Cathedral funeral of President George H. W. Bush in 2018, but then also blended his story with his substantive content in the second paragraph:

The story was almost over even before it had fully begun. Shortly after dawn on Saturday, September 2, 1944, Lieutenant Junior Grade George Herbert Walker Bush, joined by two crew mates, took off from the USS San Jacinto to attack a radio tower on Chichijima. As they approached the target, the air was heavy with flak. The plane was hit. Smoke filled the cockpit; flames raced across the wings. "My god," Lieutenant Bush thought, "this thing's gonna go down." Yet he kept the plane in its 35-degree dive, dropped his bombs, and then roared off out to sea, telling his crew mates to hit the silk. Following protocol, Lieutenant Bush turned the plane so they could bail out.

Only then did Bush parachute from the cockpit.

The wind propelled him backward, and he gashed his head on the tail of the plane as he flew through the sky. He plunged deep into the ocean, bobbed to the surface, and flopped onto a tiny raft. His head bleeding, his eyes burning, his mouth and throat raw from salt water, the future 41st president of the United States was alone.

Sensing that his men had not made it, he was overcome. He felt the weight of responsibility as a nearly physical burden. And he wept. Then, at four minutes shy of noon, a submarine emerged to rescue the downed pilot. George Herbert Walker Bush was safe. The story, his story and ours, would go on by God's grace.

Through the ensuing decades, President Bush would frequently ask, nearly daily, he'd ask himself, "Why me? Why was I spared?"

And in a sense, the rest of his life was a perennial effort to prove himself worthy of his salvation on that distant morning. To him, his life was no longer his own. There were always more missions to undertake, more lives to touch, and more love to give.

And what a headlong race he made of it all. He never slowed down.

Now, let's return to our goal of learning how to fit stories with our thesis question and principal topic. We do not want to be known as speakers who tell rambling stories unrelated to the theme and topic. I call our desired type of speaking: purposeful storytelling. Here is an example of this type of storytelling. I have delivered several speeches on the topic of the rapidly growing interest in what is called impact investing. I open my speech with a dramatic story of something that occurred very early in my career when six ski-masked gunmen infiltrated our offices and held us hostage, including their main target, a man of great wealth. I provide the audience with some interesting details that usually get them involved in the story. Then it takes a turn, because all those years ago, the main protagonist in the story turns to me and asks that I begin an effort that would measure the social impact of his investments and philanthropy in measurable return on investment.

After I tell this story and have the audience at attention, and at least interested in what comes next, I go on to relate what we did after that terrorist attack and how I see impact rolling and growing after all these years. It is all about the connector between your story and the rest of your content. You are relating the story to support your main themes. It is the story they will remember, and through it they may remember the main point of your speech. Stories include inherent memory value. Your goal here is to find your audiences walking away from your talk with something useable to retell in their own lives.

Let's think of some specific examples of where you find stories when you do not have your own to tell.

- If you were to speak about the need for advances in education, you might want to seek out stories from a school about students overcoming learning disabilities or students who had not been on a track to graduate from high school who did succeed and complete twelfth grade. You would want to find a couple students and perhaps interview them or talk to their teachers and ask why they were able to overcome this adversity. These stories would interest your audience.

- If you were delivering a talk about the virtues of solar energy, you would want to find homeowners who perhaps were previously opposed to solar and how and why they changed their opinion and now were convinced this was the right type of energy to power their houses. You do not have to use the real names of real people, but you do need to ground your stories in real-life situations.

- If you are discussing a new health care advance or methodology, it would be easy to find the stories of people who had suffered and were now successfully treated through your new discovery. That is valid. You see my point here. Relate your stories to your subject for the purpose of supporting the principal objective in your speech and illuminating it through examples. This is a fail-safe way to proceed down the path of effective public speaking.

4. State your claim or answer to the principal thesis you make.

After the story interlude during which you have fascinated and perhaps entertained your audience, it is time to wake them back up on a serious note. This is the section where you state your suggested answer to the challenge you have posed in section two. I should also state here that it may sound as if I am giving you an outline for a major three-hour address. That is not my intention. You can hit all seven cylinders of this architectural structure in a fifteen-minute speech as easily as in one that lasts an hour. Don't become overburdened by all this instruction. I am putting it out there to help you, pave the way, and make writing and giving a speech easier for you. There is nothing onerous about the process, and it will seem easy once you master a few talks using this pattern.

What do I mean by this? The audience has typically come to hear your views, your opinions on some matter or issue. Now is the time for you to unleash them. So far you have just announced your theme and illustrated it with compelling personal or researched stories. Now you take the plunge and state what you believe to be true. Taking some of our previous examples, this would mean that you now state your position somewhat like this:

- In the case of below-standard high school completion rates affecting all states, I would say that increasing the use of universally available instructional technology combined with more community policing that assures more students are in classes where they belong would improve the high school completion rate by 30 percent.
- We have been talking about the use of solar energy for home heating and cooling. I will go out on a limb here and predict that within twenty years, 30 percent of all homes in the United States will utilize solar energy for 100 percent of their household needs. Let me tell you why I think this will come to pass.
- As we think about launching new solutions to Type 2 diabetes, I am going to predict that this disease can be eliminated in roughly half all the adults suffering now, through telemedicine, applied nutritional management, weight control, and diet management.

Your claim is an arresting thought to keep the audience on a targeted plane and to keep them following the development of your message and your thought. It keeps the energy level high. This is because once you take the risk and state your personally held opinions, the opposing opinions will enter the minds of those in audience. There is little doubt that this will happen. Any audience typically represents a plethora of points of view. That is just fine. It keeps them engaged. Controversy is good.

Suppose I am sitting in your audience, and you make your claim about increasing high school graduation completion, and I am a member of law enforcement in a local community that has tried community policing as a way to get high school students in school and keep them there, and it has failed. I will want to know just how you can make it succeed. This means that the speaker and the listeners are now on the same playing field. As a speaker you have stimulated your audience in a new way; after the stories might have done that in a more emotional way, now you are using a more reasoned approach to engage them.

During political campaigns it is the challenger's requisite strategy to always suggest new solutions and to stake new propositions. These are the stock-in-trade of politicians because the only way they can gain media coverage is through proposals in which they make contentions and try to back them up with logic that could stall or fail. If their failure is pointed out, they might say that it was well worth the media coverage gained. If you are a college professor, it is your job to stimulate but not control thought, so you would make a claim to stimulate a free and open debate, letting the facts ultimately be discovered and stand for themselves.

In announcing your position or staking your claim, you are taking a degree of risk, but risk makes it fun. It also makes it incumbent on you to conduct sufficient research to fully substantiate your claim. We all have opinions. This is not just about opinions. Your claims need backup, especially if your remarks are televised, covered by the media, and are on the record. If you head an organization or are influential in a particular field, you should recognize that what you say in staking your claim may be used against you. So socialize with your team, or lawyers, or researchers so that what you have to say is bona fide and acceptable to your organization. You will also want to debate your claim in your own mind or with friendly colleagues. Never stake a claim without knowing precisely what arguments might be used against it, so if you are confronted in a talk or afterward, you will be completely prepared with your supporting answers and a rebuttal.

One time, after giving a talk at a New York hotel, I finished and was walking off stage when I spotted a woman careening toward me at full bore. My first instinct was to escape to the green room and shut the door to keep her out, and I moved in that direction. Her advance was swift, and as she got closer, I saw she had tears streaming down her cheeks. "Oh, no," I thought, "I am in serious trouble about something I said." It turned out that this woman was coming to tell me her story. What I had said in my speech about President Reagan had brought her to her feet. She now wanted to recount the story of her life and profess to me that Reagan had saved her life.

As a student in the Soviet Union, she had succeeded at her studies, earning a PhD in applied economics at Moscow University. But every night she retreated to her small room and held on to magazines in which she read about life in America. She envisioned that in America she would literally find heaven, but she had no hope of getting here. Then came the accommodation for Russian Jews that Reagan and Gorbachev had personally negotiated, allowing a certain number to immigrate to the US. She was one of those lucky enough to come to the US. She immediately secured a position at a leading investment bank and in one year made a fortune beyond what she had ever imagined. She didn't challenge my speech; she brought an unexpected and inspiring reaction.

5. Use supporting documentation and quotations from recognized sources to back up your claims and broaden your support.

In today's disruptive climate, I think this point is even more critically important, though rarely observed. The human mind has a great capacity to doubt, and some in your audience may make a strong case against your stated thesis just for the sake of competition with your ideas. You have to recognize this tendency and guard against it or face the possible distortion of your views. What could be worse is to be discredited. Then all your work on your presentation would be threatened. When you spend a serious amount of time on your speech, make absolutely certain you insert quotes from recognized sources to support your positions.

If President Trump only adhered to this precept, his support would be even wider than it is. His practice is to make generalized claims that allows his critics to have a field day. He throws them red meat constantly. I prefer to beat my competitors to the punch. Rather than say, "The economy is doing great," I might suggest, "According to the AFL-CIO and the US Chamber of Commerce, as well as the Commerce Department, there are more minorities and women at work today at higher wages than at any time in US history." Such a statement can be debated but with a thinner prospect of being discredited.

What does using facts to substantiate your claims accomplish?

- Impersonalizes your statements and thus "demilitarizes" the opposition.
- Proves your points to be accurate without having to say you are correct.
- Broadens your support to the members of the organizations you cite.
- Strengthens your point of view as being unassailable when you call on organizations for research that are not typically on your side.

For examples, let's go back to our three topics of education, alternative energy, and health care. Here are theoretical examples of how to add to and bolster your support with the goal of making your proposals airtight and supportable by the audience as well.

- Related to our view that high school completion rates can be increased by diligence on a number of fronts, we are joined by the National Education Association (NEA), which has established ambitious goals for this coming year to join us in this effort. For additional support, the national board of the PTA has stepped up to help enforce these goals in every high school in America.

- To further back up and substantiate our claim that within ten years 30 percent of all households will rely on solar energy sources, the Petroleum Industry Association accepts that solar energy will displace traditional oil and gas users at the rate we have proposed, and furthermore the US Department of Energy in coordination with the Congressional Budget Office has set forth what they consider to be realistic and attainable goals for solar energy usage very much in line with our predictions.

- The fact that disease prevention and better health care will reduce employer costs and improve employee performance is supported by the US Chamber of Commerce, which has shared its internal study with us that reveals a significant reduction in employee benefit costs to major corporations, and a US Department of Labor study recently showed that wellness in workers leads to employee job satisfaction.

There are plenty of resources from which you could quote publicly available data. What's more, if you are launching a serious campaign of some sort and are announcing it in your speech, seek the endorsement of as many organizations as possible on substantive issues; that way you can draw upon the underlying memberships of these organizations and instantly broaden the confidence your audience will have in your thesis.

6. Ask for audience engagement in the issue you have highlighted in your speech.

Closing in now on the ending of your speech, make an ask of your audience. Even if you do not need anything from them, still ask. It's a way to bring them into the heart of your presentation and engage them. Get them to invest a little of their own thought into the process you have just gone through on their behalf. Instead of asking them a question, direct them to action you would like to see them take. This might be nothing more than inviting them to learn more about your topic and directing them to conduct some research on their own.

Some examples drawn from speeches we have discussed might include:

- Now that you have seen a little of how the shark population worldwide is being winnowed, please join me in urging a more responsible approach to tuna fishing and making people more aware.
- If you are as concerned as I am about the low percentage of high school completion and graduations, please get involved in your community and seek out families with high schoolers and see what you might do to encourage their children to stay in school—maybe even volunteer to drive them there. Together we can effect change and make progress with an issue that has multiple ramifications for the future of our community.
- Thank you for your interest in character-based leadership. You might be asking what you can do to promote

more responsible leadership in your communities and our world. I would say please join me in encouraging responsible young people to understand what character-based leadership really is, first of all, and then encourage them to become leaders of a cause.

- You can see from our lecture today more about the importance of art, dance, and music and their relationship to learning science and math skills. So please support your local schools in their efforts to keep these vital learning modules, and also spread the word about the relationship of the arts in general to basic skills that will promote progress and careers in the sciences for young women and men everywhere.

If your talk is less on a cause and more on business, you can always ask for engagement from the audience in these ways:

- Now that you have learned about these investment strategies and the future economic cycles that might be ahead, let us know if you need more information about specific products or would like to talk with any member of our team. We will be available after this talk.
- If any of these energy-saving ideas resonate with you and you want to become involved in your own communities or even with properties you own and or live in, just see us later this afternoon or contact us at our site and we will be glad to talk in more depth.

And if your talk is informative but does not call for a specific response from the audience, you still want to draw the audience up close to you prior to your complete wrap-up and goodbye. For example this might be an approach:

- Before I bring my remarks to a close, I hope you will feel free to be in contact with me if you ever have any questions about the material we have covered this evening. I am sure the material may have engendered questions on your part, and I stand ready to answer them in the best way I can.
- As we begin to wrap up, let me just summarize by saying that the relationship between a speaker and an audience is a special one. Please contact me if you would like to discuss these ideas further, or let me know if you would like me to suggest further reading on our topic.

The bond you worked so hard to establish at the beginning of your talk should continue, even though you may not see these particular people ever again. You can perpetuate this bond for mutual benefit by throwing these life-lines out to them. Despite the number in your audience, a relationship is always between two people or directly between presenter and guest. There is too much value to your whole speech and its content to drop the ball near the end. Instead, keep up the energy and interest in your content through the end.

7. In your summation and closing you have one duty: to send them off with inspiration.

Now that you have reached the concluding remarks of your speech, do not slow down and do not let up on the energy or tone in your voice. It should remain bright and encouraging, while you do want to signal that you are nearing the end. The purpose is not for people to start noisily packing up to leave (we have all heard of that and perhaps have done it ourselves) but just the opposite—that they listen even more intently to your last words and savor them. These might be the only words they remember from the talk. They might have slept all the way through but are awakened by their companion or seat mate when the signal comes that you are wrapping up. Don't laugh. I have seen it happen in my speeches.

There are just two possible routes to an effective closing. One is to tell a short story that sums up the whole of what you have attempted to convey. The other is to focus on a short inspirational statement from a historic or contemporary figure, although you might want to include a reference to the person's qualifications if they are unknown. Your principal goal is to end on a high note. You want them to be glad they spent the hour with you, or glad they listened to you in some remote format. Remember the title of this book. The design is to help you win your audience, not lose them, when they walk away or unplug from your talk.

To accomplish that, a lot rests on the conclusion, just as much as your opening. If they have not been sold on the main body of your talk, this is a moment to reclaim them and bring them back into the winners' circle. Whether you deliver your talk extemporaneously or from notes, please remember to solidly plan your ending. You can modify or edit spontaneously as the end requires, but have a plan. This is critical. It doesn't matter if your talk is ten minutes or fifty. You will always need an opening and a conclusion. Don't squander either.

If you select the first route of summarizing your talk, do it by starting this way: "There are three things I hope you will take away from this brief talk..." or "What would I like you to remember from our time together today? Here are four things." If you use this approach, never employ more than four points. If you do, it might tax the patience of the members in the audience who are ready to pole-vault to the next event. Then make your summary points very brief, not more than one sentence, and memorable—perhaps even rhyming or poetic.

You might also choose to send them out with just one thought in summation of your talk. If you go that route, you need to make it a big-deal point and make it powerful but poignant and obviously related to the whole focus of the presentation. Let's say you are giving a lecture on the life of the great architect Frank Lloyd Wright and you want to summarize in one point. You might say, "It has been enjoyable for me to share with you a little about life of this iconic architect of invention, and I would like you to remember just one thing about this great man: He left us a legacy of modernism to follow and enhanced our appreciation of our own habitats in a way no other American architect has."

Or let's say you are giving a talk about the history and impact of the baseball great Jackie Robinson. You might summarize and send out your guests this way: "It has been an honor to share with you some of the struggles and triumphs of this pioneer and pathfinder in American sports. If you remember anything about Jackie Robinson from what we learned together tonight, remember that his legacy lives on in every game that is played today, in every baseball stadium, and with every team, and every player. What he accomplished will never be erased!"

If your tone is more thoughtful and relating to self-help or encouragement, you could use a quote from someone like Henry Drummond, who wrote this beautiful sentiment: *"You will find that as you look back on your life that the moments where you have truly lived are the moments when you have done things in the spirit of Love."*

There is no shortage of inspirational quotes to be found on Google or in books you might read or in speeches you hear or in the lives of your friends and family. Your only requirement in selecting one is to make sure it inspires you. Otherwise it could seem gratuitous.

In thinking of send-offs and goodbyes, the best example I can give you is how Carol Burnett said goodbye every time she ended her long-running hour-long televised variety show. Her closing routine, which is the way you should think of your speech ending, has become iconic. If you did not watch the *Carol Burnett Show* or its reruns because you are too young, then find them on YouTube. Watch a couple of the endings. Of course, the music, which you will not necessarily have access to as a speaker, adds emotion to the special feeling of it, but still you can see how she comes out and simply says how special it has been to be...*together*! There in one word is what I want you to know and feel.

Carol is the best example of an actor who knew how to bring down the fourth wall. In fact, with her, the fourth wall never even went up. She was just playing with you up there on stage, acting foolish, just the way you feel sometimes. She always made fun of our foibles, failings, idiosyncrasies, and above all our humanness. We may have been watching thousands of miles away and she was acting in a studio in Los Angeles, but when she says good night, she says we have been together. And it's not a stretch for us, because we feel it. That is the goal and the hope I have for you in every speech you give. Your ending is your way to seal it.

CHAPTER TEN

The Physical Delivery of Your Message

Your content is metaphysical.
Your delivery is physical.
Don't let your words get in the way of your speaking.

Getting Started: Essential Tips for Preparing Your Speech Text

Here are five critical steps that will help you physically type or write your content in ways that promote successful speaking. I think you will appreciate and employ these small but critically important details.

1. If you write out your remarks, or even make an outline or notes to guide your presentation, make absolutely sure that you write your content colloquially. That means to write it how you speak it. This is your own unique voice. Make the words conform to how

you speak—not how you write. Do not use the same language you would use for publication or even a business email or letter. For example, when speaking we almost always use contractions. Make sure you write for speaking this way as well. When speaking we might not always obey rules about periods or other punctuation if they get in the way of a smooth and natural delivery. In a way, you can disobey your grammar teachers and write in what I call "talking language." You might come closer to the way texting is written today. Just so long as you don't make it so clipped that it is difficult for you to translate what you need to say from what you have written.

Your sentence structure for speaking may be fluid and include lots of dashes for breaks in word flow. You will use parenthesis or brackets to help you with pausing or phrasing. Your script for speaking is just that; it is not a text for an academic paper to be published. Type it out with the goal of readability and ease. You may add marks or notes in your own handwriting. It may look messy, and that is acceptable as long as it does not confuse you. Do not ask anyone else to do this or to touch your manuscript. Only you can do this— read your own script and make sense of it.

Make absolute certain you read your script out loud prior to delivery. You will be surprised at how many errors you catch and how you need to smooth it out for speaking. Do not count on putting something on paper that will be perfect when you speak it. You will need to continuously edit. Make certain you practice out loud. When you deliver the speech, it should not be the first time you have spoken it out loud.

Would you like to see the script that a president or head of state speaks from? It is completely marked up with underlining and proper emphasis and with difficult to pronounce names and foreign words phonetically written out. It would never pass an editor's red pencil test. There will be marks all over the place, and it will make sense only to the speaker. There is zero tolerance for embarrassing mistakes or mispronunciations or poor timing. What is released to the media is a different and cleaned-up version. This is your own playbook and personal version. It should become an old friend to you, and you should become completely comfortable with it.

2. If you use abbreviations for words in your written copy or notes, make certain that when you are at the podium, you are not stumped by your shorthand notes or scribbles. I have had this happen to me. In my haste I have used abbreviations such as *WH* for White House or *Tues* for Tuesday, and for the life of me, when I get rolling making a speech, these references could appear as strange as Greek to me. I have told you that while you are speaking, many thoughts and ideas will flow through your brain—most just tedious things that come from nowhere. You can get distracted. Consider my own recent example.

I was in the middle of a talk when, as I was cruising along, I started looking for a specific note on what

I was to say, and it was missing—it had vanished. Fortunately, I knew the script by heart but did not really trust myself. It became a small mental wrestling match in the recesses of my mind that distracted me right in the middle of the presentation. I don't think my audience noticed, but I surely did! That was lax preparation. If you make notes or cues to yourself, make absolutely sure they are in the right place when and where you need them to be. Also, it's much better to write out any words fully instead of using their abbreviation. That is like life insurance.

3. Type or print your talk in at least a fourteen- or sixteen-point font in a serif style on one side of the paper only. Not two-sided. It is easier to read this way. Err on the side of making it larger than you think you need. Don't worry if someone sees your copy. So what? You are smart to have it appear in large type. You will be grateful you did, when one eye gets blurry, you forgot your reading glasses, or the lights are dim. Use black ink on white hard-milled paper, not laid or textured paper. Keep your text centered on the page with wide margins, so that if you read it your eyes will not dart left and right but up or down. This is the way teleprompters work. If you can make your presentation from notes or use your printed talk as a guide, keeping the text running down the center of the page will also be useful. Double-spacing is good for the format.

If you wear glasses or contacts, make sure, if you are on a trip, that you have a second pair available somewhere. Always carry a pen or pencil with you to make last-minute corrections. You may use a yellow or other color highlighter, especially if you are referring mostly to key points. Just remember to affirm to yourself why you have highlighted those sections. It's amazing what you will forget with a lot going on around you.

I like to use eight-and-a-half-by-eleven-inch paper for a text because I can fold it down the middle and place it inside my interior coat pocket. A woman may have to carry it in hand or a portfolio. NUMBER YOUR PAGES! Top and bottom. Do you know how many people I work with who do not? Paper clip your pages on one copy and staple a second copy, and carry two with you at all times. If you drop or tear the one that is clipped, you will always be able to depend on the one that is stapled. It is preferable to read from or refer to pages you can place one behind the other discreetly as you go through your speech rather than using the stapled version and having to flip the pages. It's distracting and makes the audience wonder just how many more pages to go until you are finished! The pages on the podium should be as invisible to the audience as possible. If they see what looks to them like a ream of paper, and I have seen this happen, they will start to panic, thinking they may be trapped in the lecture for hours.

Large, white five-by-eight-inch non-ruled plain index cards may be used, but they are messy to handle and can be dropped or lost. I have seen this happen. It is hard to recover the confidence of your audience afterward—even though you might attempt to make a joke about it. The three-by-five-inch cards are just too small. Also keep a clean, finished copy of the speech on your laptop or phone. If you only speak from notes on your phone, you are running a risk. I know there are people who do this regularly without a problem, so by all means stick with a successful practice. Just make sure you do not run low on power and that there is a reliable wireless network to connect to. You could end up like Bill Clinton who, twice during his presidency, had the wrong speech projected in front of him on a teleprompter at the State of the Union; he had to ad lib until the operators corrected the error. (I wonder if they had a job the next day when they went to work!) If you travel with an associate, make certain they have a copy of your remarks in their hands or on their device.

4. If you are mentioning proper names of individuals, cities, countries, rivers, historical documents or anything remotely difficult to pronounce, by all means write it out phonetically. Google has a verbal pronunciation tool so you never need to be incorrect. One practical exercise, utilized by news readers, is to learn the correct pronunciation and then walk around the house or office and say the name over and over aloud, so when you speak it, it rolls off your tongue effortlessly and correctly. If you are wrong, it shows a lack of attention to detail and could bring you down a notch in the minds of the listeners. If you are uncertain even after checking with Google (which is not always perfect either), then ask your local host if they can help you with it. You will get credit for asking. Likewise, if you are speaking in a town or area that has an unusual name or you are thanking individuals with complex names, check the correct pronunciations.

If you are speaking in a foreign country and you have the idea that you would like to speak a few words of welcome in the native language of your audience, make sure you have a native speaker as a tutor. I issue a slight warning about this. To assume you can easily learn to speak even in the proper dialect of the country's language in a region where you are speaking is a tall order, one that I have seen go wrong. If you generally have a facility for language, then by all means go with it, and even if you get it slightly wrong you may receive credit for trying. When John F. Kennedy made his successful trip to Berlin and proclaimed "Ich bin ein Berliner," he won hearts and minds everywhere.

If you are speaking in a government setting or in an official capacity where protocol is observed, research how officials or royalty are to be addressed. There are specific rules, and in some countries, not adhering to them is a serious mistake and considered rude behavior. Learning to speak according to protocol is not impossible to accomplish, and it reveals your genuine interest in and respect for your audience and a graciousness that will win you points and possibly help you if negotiations are involved.

5. Once you have your content in clear and understandable shape, you may begin to make marks in the margin. These are summary tools to lead you onward throughout your document. If you are giving this same speech several times, these helpers in the margins will assist you in moving away from reading your script and toward using only the notes. It will also help you to add spontaneous or timely remarks that may not be in the formal text. That's the way I do it. After you have given a talk on a specific subject several times, on subsequent times you may be able to just follow the notes in the margins for a more informal approach. Make use of them.

You may also elect to make other marks in the script that indicate where you may want to add a story you have more recently heard about or to add a name of someone you just met. Make these insertions now to help with the flow and to be useful as you begin to move away from the strict text and to give your talk only referring to notes or from memory. The more comfortable you are with your content, as you have laid it out on paper, the easier it is to visualize, which is the main road to memorization or giving the speech completely free of the printed document.

Adding Emphasis, Rhythm, Cadence to Your Speech

English is a relatively new language and one that is an amalgamation of Germanic, French, Latin, and other languages, created by migrants and conquerors who landed in what is now Britain. As the language developed over generations, the written and spoken version of the language diverged. Putting dialects aside and formalizing what the British call "the Queen's English" took centuries of education and standardization, and came about largely due to the beginning of the publishing and printing industries. For many of us whose native language is English, it nevertheless remains an unending educational process to learn to speak it fluently and correctly.

There are many dialects in England, Australia, and the US. Some are regional, some ethnic, some religious, and some reflect our educational level. Some people speak English with what we would call an affectation or highbrow approach, while others prefer a working-class colloquial version. There is nothing wrong with speaking using a dialect or accent; in fact personally, I think it makes a speech more interesting. It is important, however, not to give up being understood through the mispronunciation or incorrect emphasis in words you use for your talks. If you know or have been told that some audiences might not clearly understand your speaking inflection, work on getting that fixed right away. Your ideas, work, and thoughts are too valuable to waste on words not heard or understood by your audience. If you rap your message, you are likely to see signs of delight from the audience but they might not be able to recite for you precisely what your message was. One of the greatest gifts we have is the ability to give expression to our thoughts through language and speaking, and we need to continually prize and polish that gift.

The next step after editing your speech is to add emphasis, phrasing, and cadence notes to it. This is an absolute requirement for the best speakers, because expressing words constructed in sentences fluently is rarely a natural, God-given skill.

Correct Emphasis

Correct emphasis is critical to learn because it delivers meaning and understanding to your principal ideas. Correct emphasis can change everything for the listener. It is well worth the effort to learn, and you will be highly praised for more clearly understandable and articulated speeches if you express yourself with correct emphasis.

The principles of emphasis are not random. There are rules. The rules work. Once you learn proper emphasis, it will be hard for you to listen to people who are only making a guess on what words are important to stress in a sentence. Those speakers who are the hardest for me to listen to are the ad readers on local radio. They might be advertising a new roof or gutters, but they never seem to know what words to emphasize and often go right for the pronouns like YOU, THEM, HER, and these are rarely the ones to stress. Let's examine a few useful rules and get more clarity on how to speak correctly to enhance our content and message.

Primary emphasis is on words in any sentence that you will stress with either an upward inflection or a downward inflection or exclamation. The general rule is that you primarily stress, for example, especially the first time they appear in a sentence:

Nouns, adjectives, adverbs
Proper names
Cities, countries, towns

Verbs rarely get the emphasis, but can on some occasions. Subdued or non-emphasized words or phrases might be old ideas (already mentioned in previous sentences or passages) or do not materially affect the meaning of the sentence.

Sentences, like thoughts, are related to one another. The same word repeated in a second sentence may be subdued because it is being repeated and is an "old" idea once used already. A simple example might be the one cited below. In this case you should underline in your text the emphasized word and add a little upward or downward arrow at the end of the word. In this example both emphasized words share an upward inflection. All the other words are subdued.

Today I drove to the country *market*. Tomorrow I may visit *another* market.

Now to add comparisons to these two sentences let's add another feature, in this case illustrated by stressing *today*, compared with *tomorrow*. So read it now.

Today I drove to the country *market*. *Tomorrow* I may visit *another* market.

Now to add emphasis through proper phrasing, let's add a slash or a break this way.

Today/I drove to the country *market*. *Tomorrow*/I may visit *another* market.

Now let's add our means of conveyance to the sentence and see where we go with it.

Today/I drove to the country *market* by *car. Tomorrow*/I may visit *another* market on *foot.*

Notice that we did not emphasize any verbs or personal pronouns, so that the meaning came through clearly and was not confusing. You can test it by seeing if you could ascertain the meaning without reading the subdued words.

Today/market/car. Tomorrow/another/foot.

Subduing is really my favorite law because it quiets down the flow of words and eliminates all but the most essential to hear and, through subduing, the right words then get more prominent play—and these are generally the "meaning" words.

The way you might help yourself with subduing part of a sentence could be to cross out lightly with a pencil the phrase, or you could put it in parentheses.

For example:

Today/(I drove to the country market) by *car. Tomorrow*/(I may visit) *another* (market) on *foot.*

There are other laws of emphasis to be taught and learned, but they are better explained in person. You can find more lessons about emphasis on YouTube or other sources. Just remember how important emphasis is, especially if you have a complicated or conceptual or technical speech to give. Any speech, however plain and direct, can be helped significantly if you know the laws of proper emphasis.

Rhythm and Cadence

Rhythm and cadence are the ways you add grace to your talk. Think of it this way: when you hear a song being sung, really in any style, you are really hearing a type of speech. Very often the words make sense, have meaning, convey emotion, and get a reaction or response from the audience. Isn't that what you seek as a presenter as well? You want to think about making the lines of your speech a lyrical expression. One definition of *lyrical* as it relates to giving a speech is "expressing the writer's emotion in an imaginative and beautiful way." I like that. When you think lyrically about your speech and the way you give it, you are adding polish, and an extra benefit accrues from your effort.

Each person has their own individual cadence when speaking naturally, and as it relates to public speaking, your cadence is driven by the content of your speech and directly affects the quality of your delivery. If you listen to the content of your speech and you hear an urgent or dramatic message, you may accelerate your emphasis, rhythm, or breathing to express urgency, not in a dramatic way and yet to express it with a more energetic cadence. Let's call this *content cadence*. This would be rhythm driven by the meaning of what you are conveying. If you come to a point in your content where you are telling a story about people being trapped in a fire or trapped in illiteracy or trapped by tyranny, you would not express this with the same cadence as you would if you were reading a grocery list. Public speaking is not dramatic oration, but it is not devoid of drama either.

When your speech includes a narrative or has quotations of specific words spoken by characters, you will not assume a dramatic posture but nonetheless you will hasten the cadence or slow it down depending on the content of the narrative and the need to add pauses. In some ways cadence is also your own unique inflection. Not everyone finds this, due to a lack of authenticity. The Kennedys had it, perhaps largely helped by their Boston accents. You knew they were talking when you heard their voices. This was of course also true of Churchill and Reagan to some extent. Oprah has it, and of course Dr. King had it in abundance. Individual and iconic cadence cannot be pretentious or fake. Governor Mario Cuomo had it. He was a dramatic and fluid speaker. It has to come naturally, but once achieved, your speeches are especially memorable and you may be more sought after as a speaker.

Let's look here at a few more lines from Dr. King's famous "Mountaintop" speech in which it was said he predicted his death the following day, and think about cadence, as he was the master of it. We do not desire to copy him but to learn the value as applied to our own unique cadence as we express it through our own unique messages.

Something is happening in Memphis; something is happening in our world. And you know, if I were standing at the beginning of time, with the possibility of taking a kind of general and panoramic view of the whole of human history up to now, and the Almighty said to me, "Martin Luther King, which age would you like to live in?" I would take my mental flight by Egypt and I would watch God's children in their magnificent trek from the dark dungeons of Egypt through, or rather across the Red Sea, through the wilderness on toward the promised land. And in spite of its magnificence, I wouldn't stop there.

I would move on by Greece and take my mind to Mount Olympus. And I would see Plato, Aristotle, Socrates, Euripides and Aristophanes assembled around the Parthenon. And I would watch them around the Parthenon as they discussed the great and eternal issues of reality. But I wouldn't stop there.

I would go on, even to the great heyday of the Roman Empire. And I would see developments around there, through various emperors and leaders. But I wouldn't stop there.

I would even come up to the day of the Renaissance and get a quick picture of all that the Renaissance did for the cultural and aesthetic life of man. But I wouldn't stop there.

I would even go by the way that the man for whom I am named had his habitat. And I would watch Martin Luther as he tacked his ninety-five theses on the door at the church of Wittenberg. But I wouldn't stop there.

I would come on up even to 1863 and watch a vacillating president by the name of Abraham Lincoln finally come to the conclusion that he had to sign the Emancipation Proclamation. But I wouldn't stop there.

I would even come up to the early thirties, and see a man grappling with the problems of the bankruptcy of his nation. And come with an eloquent cry that we have nothing to fear but "fear itself." But I wouldn't stop there.

Strangely enough, I would turn to the Almighty, and say, "If you allow me to live just a few years in the second half of the twentieth century, I will be happy."

CHAPTER ELEVEN

The Winning Send-Off

Never Lose Control

You have undertaken your speech or made your pitch because you want to win. You want to earn new business, name recognition, more book sales, more credibility, more attention on a national or international crisis or philanthropy. You may need to defend your reputation, promote a stock offering, answer questions in a court of law, or conduct a high-stakes media interview or just make a sales call on a phone. You may want to give the best lecture you can to a college class or make the best pitch for investment dollars. It's all about winning through persuasion. It's all about using the skills you have gained in this book. Now it's time to put them to the test.

For the speaker-audience relationship to thrive right up until you say thank you and goodbye, the speaker has to retain and maintain control of the presentation through to the end. Your content and the delivery are your complete responsibility. Keep your energy level high and check in with yourself to make certain it is not lagging near the conclusion. Write a little note to yourself saying, "KEEP ENERGY LEVEL UP" and stick it on the podium. This means keeping your voice pitch and tone assertive as well. I have heard speakers lower their voice near their conclusion. That doesn't work. The powerful ending will be remembered.

You can win by the quality and high note of your ending. If your presentation up until this last pitch has been tepid or lacked passion—you have one more chance at bat. Give it your finest. Most in the audience will remember more about what you say in closing than other parts of your talk. When you begin to draw your remarks to a close is often when people start to take particular note. When asked by their parents, friends, professors, what they remember from your talk, more than you might expect they will refer to your ending. "Great wrap-up!" they'll say. You may have struggled a bit to gain traction during the main body of the speech. Now you have time to redeem yourself. Leave the very best for last.

You are the performer, actor, presenter, and responsible party, especially as most speeches or talks are arranged and given for some purpose. This could be to advance the programming of a club, association, university, school, or company; or to provide an income to the speaker or to enhance their reputation and support book sales or a special personal brand or products. As a result, the speaker is typically rewarded in some monetary or non-monetary way for the work undertaken to prepare and deliver a talk. This all implies ownership and responsibility. You may have had help and coaching, but at last you are alone with your message and your audience. No one else can do this work for you.

I have only ever heard one person, emboldened by fame and

extreme arrogance, show up on the podium without a prepared talk and start by saying "Okay. I'm here. Do you have any questions?" There was no attempt to prepare, and interestingly, there was a big fee being paid to the speaker. As it happened I was also on the program and had worked assiduously on my remarks and was being paid a great deal less, I am sure, than the person who basically just showed up. I will never forget that. Perhaps his celebrity entitled him to behave that way. It was interesting, though, to observe the outright value, to some audiences, of fame. I could not take anything away from him in that category for sure.

In some cases, you will have a contract and in others just an invitation. In either case make certain you have carefully reviewed your obligations and if necessary, have your attorney do so as well. If you are representing your employer or merely an employed individual speaking on your own, you may need to clear your content or sign a disclaimer that releases you from the official business of your employer.

In all cases where you are employed and you are speaking, make certain that you are fully briefed by your employer and that you understand the legal ramifications of speaking in public about certain investments or prohibited information related to corporate status involving mergers, sale, items affecting the valuation of public companies, disclosure of information in organizations where you have signed nondisclosure agreements, and basically wherever your remarks could be construed as representing a third party or might be disparaging or promotive of them without their permission.

On the other hand, if you are an official corporate spokesperson, you will surely be speaking on behalf of the interests of the firm, and you will need to be fully informed about your limitations in this role as well. You will need to be careful about providing private information, even in the interest of the firm, to journalists and investors. There is professional training available for investor relations professionals, which I strongly urge you to undertake. To protect yourself I would always suggest recording your comments if you are giving a speech about your firm so that there is always transparency and you are protected officially in case someone should misquote you for their own interests. Never yield control.

Questions and Answers

Whenever possible avoid a question-and-answer session, during or following your presentation. If you are thinking that it might be an easy way to get out of preparing too much material by relying on a good and lengthy Q & A session, forget that strategy.

Here are six reasons why you should not plan on or announce a Q & A segment as well as a suggestion about a better approach.

1. If you end your main speech and turn it over to the audience, you have thrown away your control of the message completely, and in an instant, you have lost command of the podium.

2. Your ending, as I have explained earlier, is one of your most important segments—to send people away enlightened,

inspired, or ready to take action. By introducing a new segment, you throw all that goodwill out the window.

3. I can guarantee you that at least 75 percent of all questioners want to stand and make a point rather than really ask you a genuine question. Even genuine questions can turn the whole focus on end and can sour the audience on you and your topic.

4. This type of session can invite confrontation. You have yielded the gavel, and your host may have to step in.

5. Imagine that while you are answering one question, you have basically left the rest of the audience out and you are focusing on one person. Not good. There is also the problem with sound. By all means make certain you repeat the question and scan the whole audience with your eyes, arms, and body and make sure that while the question may have been asked by one person, you are answering to everyone in the room—that is if you are absolutely required to participate in this type of forum.

6. A better way to handle this is to suggest, prior to your final wrap-up, that you will gladly remain at the front of the room or in the lobby and answer any and all questions as best you can after you conclude.

There are, of course, exceptions to this rule. When the crowd is very small, intimate, known to each other, Q & A can be personal, warm, and fun. I have given talks at private homes when there might be, say, twenty-five or thirty people present. It's natural and accommodating to allow questions then. They are less likely to be hostile or grandstanding. Another time might be with students. I have given talks in classrooms or with small conferences where a part of the purpose of a talk is to help those present dig into greater detail that can only be acquired through targeted questions. It may even be a part of their assignment, and they might have to write a paper or take an exam about your subject. The same can also be true at bookstores, where there are small gatherings and people want to engage the author—that may be the whole reason they attend.

When I have given a talk remotely on Zoom or Skype, I usually accept questions because it is tedious to be talking so long with a remote audience where there is too little personal interaction. There is one more situation when this is obviously allowable, and that is when Q & A is mandated by the host organization as something that is always done, by tradition. I would not fight that tradition. I would yield and go along with it.

If you do conduct these sessions, please make every attempt to maintain control of the time and manage it yourself, being aware that it will surely be tedious for some in the audience and even irritating for some to hear their friends or foes ask questions. Keep the session under a strict time limit, which you should announce at the start. And most important, end on a high note. If you get a good question and you are near the time to end, then by all means do so. Try not to end when the question or an answer has not been upbeat or positive.

If the questions have been controversial or even hostile, it is important to remember two things:

1. When you end the session, do it decisively! If someone shouts an additional question or demands a better answer, if you have called the session closed, then mean it and stick with your decision to cut it off. It is not fair to others to keep a session running for just one or a few questioners.

2. Remember, despite the fact that you may have been brought up, as I was, to answer a question asked of you, you can reverse this rule now. Just because someone asks you a question does not mean you have to answer it. The best way to handle it is not to say, "I will not answer that" but to provide an answer to a more general question or one that is slightly off in a related but different direction. The strategy here is that you remain in control of the topic. If you are smart and quick enough to do so, you might also be able to deflect the tension through humor. Just remember, though, that this is a high-risk strategy that can backfire, because people can also take humor personally, so make it light.

Finally, never end this type of session without two things: remind your audience of the inspirational quote you ended with and your hope that they will go out and use the information they learned during your talk, and then also thank them for being a good audience and tell them you hope to see them again soon. This is your time to repair the rift in your connection with the entire audience and bring your relationship completely home again with all participants.

Hecklers, Protestors, Disagreeables

If you are a public office holder or a corporate leader representing a company that might be under some type of attention
in the media or, as we have discussed before, a speaker on a
college campus, you may be confronted by people who seek to
challenge you, embarrass you, or draw attention to you or to a
related controversy. They might also try to subvert and reach
your assembled audience with their own opinions and messages. The most important thing to recognize is that as long
as these disrupters are orderly and you are in a public place,
they are protected by law. If the challengers are a part of the
invited or paying audience already, they are there purposely
and strategically. If you are speaking at a private venue, security can remove them and your host organization should know
what to do. If you think this might happen, make your plans
in advance.

If your challenger is taunting you or asking you questions
for the sake of provoking or starting a controversy, perhaps to
generate media attention, it is critical you do not take the bait.
Your job is to remain passive and not to respond or escalate the
interruption. Escalating could make a bigger issue out of the
interruption than it might be if you remain quiet and calm and
do not react. If you or your host organization are aware prior
to your talk that there may be interrupters, it is important that
you let law enforcement or security know and ask them to be
on hand for the event. These incidents are their responsibility,
not yours. They will also direct you not to provoke any protestors or respond to their interruptions at all.

The Outcome Is Your Responsibility

After all the many elements of the job description for a speaker we have discussed, it may seem onerous to you. The training and coaching, the content, the audience relationship, the travel, the host relationship, the performance, the production responsibilities—you may feel that public speaking is more complicated than you had thought. I have given you a full range of all the possible features that need to be addressed and managed as a speaker, and it is true that the buck stops with you. If your speech is not effective or you are interrupted or you have planned the wrong message for the audience or you are nervous, it all accrues to you.

From the audience perspective, it appears that the speaker breezes in without a care in the world and that it is relatively easy to make a presentation. Of course, I have taken on the most serious aspects of serious speech-making. If you are in a position where you have a team devoted to scheduling, speech-writing, travel, advance, arrangements—as some people do—it may relieve you of many of the things we have talked about; however, being aware of all it takes and all that goes into making a successful presentation is important, I think, because appreciating all that it takes will give you a humility that is attractive and attracting to your audience.

Leave the Audience Wanting More

By all means do not conclude your remarks by letting your audience feel that you have given all you've got. Hold back a little. Be a little mysterious and slightly aloof. You might draw your remarks to a close with a line like this:

> *I have so much more I would like to cover with you and so many more stories to share, but I know our time together is limited, so I will have to start wrapping this up.*

Your highest honor and proof that you have won is that you are invited back, or if you are a salesperson, that you have made the sale. I have a friend who is a college professor. I have heard him lecture to groups. I can honestly say he is on fire about his topics and makes you want much more from him. Standing ovations are everyday fare for him, and he has been voted most popular lecturer on campus for three years! Just as I am writing this about him, my excitement level is rising about the next time I will hear him.

Just as you conclude with this statement about having more you would like to cover, I sometimes begin by stating:

> *I have so much I want to share with you tonight I am not sure we will be able to get through everything in our allotted time, but I will try.*

Starting this way also gives your audience an idea that you have a lot to give and makes them excited at the prospect. You can convey this in webinars and online appearances as well. I am not suggesting a strategy of self-promotion. No. I am suggesting that you share your honest enthusiasm about your content and message. This is not about you. It is about what you have to say on this subject or others and are willing to share. Remember if you tell your audience a secret, they will bond with you. You could say:

> *In closing, I want to share something with you that I rarely reveal about what is going on in the country right now, according to my observation...*

Of course, the precise best way to be invited back or to win a second follow-up sales call is to come across as knowledgeable about something your audiences want to learn more about. If you come across as smart and having valuable information, which is different than saying you are smart, you may end with cheers of MORE! MORE!

Empower and Inspire the Audience to Act

The very best way to conclude your talk is to provide your audience with tools, a road map, a plan, supporting documentation, data, examples, critical information, and ways to put all this to use on their own behalf. Reagan often implored his audience to do more and to be more heroic. He expected the audience to do something as a result of his talk. He was the kind of leader who made you want to be better, do more, rise to your better self. He revealed that in his speeches through examples of heroic people he admired. His trick was that he was never the one telling you to be better, it was the lives of his heroic historic figures he told you about that made you want to be better and live a life that mattered.

Reagan's favorite way to end a speech was often to repeat the famous call of the American patriot Thomas Paine who said: *"We have it in our power to begin the world over again."*

Leave Them Smarter, Inspired, and Glad They Came

We should remember that the greatest speeches may not be the ones that send men and women to war or to the moon or mark a new technological advance. A great speech might use the simplest language but carry the most emotion, may be honest and blunt but stir the greatest indignation, or deploy the most logic and convince an influential gathering to take up a cause.

Most who are schooled in oratory and speech-giving rank the same historical speeches of the past as the greatest of all time. Where are the great speeches of today? In many ways I think you could find them anywhere and everywhere, given by children, teachers, musicians, artists—anyone called upon to do so. Among the finest speeches I hear today are those delivered from the remarkable and heroic police spokespeople who have to go on live television and explain violence that happens in their communities to people around the world. I remember hearing these people who are mostly not professionally trained speakers in places like Dallas, Las Vegas, Charleston, and Manchester, England. It seems because they are among those hurting the most, they have the most to say, and they know they must say it with dignity and honesty because they are speaking for many who have been silenced.

Honesty and storytelling, humility and genuineness rule the day, and this is what sends your audience home happy and grateful for having listened to you.

Here is my favorite example of a speech that is honored as one of the greatest but is surely one of the simplest. Its power is from what it stands for, and it is breathtaking for its plainness, brevity, and emotion. It was given on the retirement of the baseball great Lou Gehrig, due to his illness. Here it is in its brief entirety:

> *Fans, for the past two weeks you have been reading about the bad break I got. Yet today I consider myself the luckiest man on the face of this earth. I have been in ballparks for seventeen years and have never received anything but kindness and encouragement from you fans.*
>
> *Look at these grand men. Which of you wouldn't consider it the highlight of his career just to associate with them for even one day? Sure, I'm lucky. Who wouldn't consider it an honor to have known Jacob Ruppert? Also, the builder of baseball's greatest empire, Ed Barrow? To have spent six years with that wonderful little fellow, Miller Huggins? Then to have*

spent the next nine years with that outstanding leader, that smart student of psychology, the best manager in baseball today, Joe McCarthy? Sure, I'm lucky.

When the New York Giants, a team you would give your right arm to beat, and vice versa, sends you a gift—that's something. When everybody down to the groundskeepers and those boys in white coats remember you with trophies—that's something. When you have a wonderful mother-in-law, who takes sides with you in squabbles with her own daughter—that's something. When you have a father and a mother who work all their lives so you can have an education and build your body—it's a blessing. When you have a wife who has been a tower of strength and shown more courage than you dreamed existed—that's the finest I know.

So, I close in saying that I may have had a tough break, but I have an awful lot to live for.

Lou Gehrig was a heroic man who told his dramatic and sad story with simple heartfelt words and they reached the hearts of everyone who heard them.

Acknowledgments

This book would not have been conceived and written if I had not been trained in communication from two important people in my life. First, my dad, Kenneth Rosebush, whose currency was found in new ideas; whose fearlessness came from embracing change; whose inspiration came from music; and satisfaction from teaching people how to communicate. And second, my boss, President Ronald Reagan, whose examples of soaring rhetoric and soul-infused oratory led me down deeper paths of inquiry and commitment to helping people understand the power of words and their delivery. I am humbled by what I learned from both men and grateful they deemed me worthy of being their student.

In addition, my most sincere gratitude goes to my wife, Nancy Rosebush, who, as a professional editor herself, tirelessly worked to improve this book. And to Adrien Yule, whose insight as a classical speech coach contributed to my own view of this topic. And to my friend James F. Caughman, a devoted student of rhetoric and language, whose suggestions have increased the value of this book.

Index